Literature Circles
through Technology

Terence W. Cavanaugh

Professional Development Resources for
K-12 Library Media and Technology Specialists

Microsoft screenshots reprinted with permission from Microsoft Corporation.

Adobe product screen shots reprinted with permission from Adobe Systems Inc.

eReader product screen shots reprinted with permission from eReader.

Figure 3.16 reprinted with permission from International Children's Digital Library.
Figure 3.17 reprinted with permission from Jim Write.
Figure 5.3 reprinted with permission from Caroline S. Parr, at Central Rappahannock Regional Library, Fredericksburg, VA.
Figure 5.4 reprinted with permission from Kaline Goodrich at Nancy Keane.
Figure 5.5 reprinted with permission from Marcelo Bursztein at ePALS Classroom Exchange.
Figure 5.6 reprinted with permission from Lynn Davis at Roselle Public Library, Roselle, IL.
Figure 5.8 reprinted with permission from Elizabeth Amared at Google.
Figure 5.10 reprinted with permission from Elizabeth Amared at Google/Blogger.
Figure 5.11 reprinted with permission from Matt Mullenweg at *m@mullenweg.com*.
Figure 6.4 reprinted with permission from Scholastic.
Figure 6.5 reprinted with permission from Mike Richardson at TWICE.
Figure 6.3, 6.7, 6.8, and 6.9, reprinted with permission from Blackboard.
Figure 6.9 reprinted with permission from author Casey Porter.
ISTE NETS reprinted with permission from Maddelyn High at ISTE.
Information Power information reprinted with permission from ALA.

Library of Congress Cataloging-in-Publication Data

Cavanaugh, Terence W.
  Literature circles through technology / Terence Cavanaugh.
      p. cm.
  Includes bibliographical references and index.
  ISBN 1-58683-203-4 (pbk.)
  1. Group reading--Technological innovations. 2. Book clubs (Discussion groups)--Technological innova-
tions. 3. Literature--Study and teaching--Technological innovations. 4. Student-centered learning--
Technological innovations. I. Title.
LC6631.C38 2006
374.22--dc22
                                         2006003200

Published by Linworth Publishing, Inc.
480 East Wilson Bridge Road, Suite L
Worthington, Ohio 43085

ISBN: 1-58683-203-4

5 4 3 2 1

Table of Contents

Table of Contents continued

Table of Contents continued

Table of Figures

Table of Figures *continued*

Table of Tables

About the Author

Dr. Terence Cavanaugh is a visiting assistant professor in curriculum and instruction, teaching educational technology at the University of North Florida's College of Education and Human Services. With degrees in science education and instructional technology, his areas of expertise include curriculum development, instructional technology, assistive technology, and teacher education. In addition to his college-level experience, Dr. Cavanaugh has more than fifteen years of teaching experience at the middle and high school levels. He taught science and technology in the United States, the Caribbean, and the Middle East, and has developed educational technology materials for organizations integrating technology and curriculum, distance education, and methods for teaching special needs learners.

Acknowledgements

Many thanks to my wife, Dr. Cathy Cavanaugh, for all of her patience, understanding, and assistance through late nights and weekends spent working on this project. I am also deeply appreciative of educators throughout Florida who were excited by, participated in, and provided valuable feedback concerning these technology-integrated literature circle activities.

Introduction

Literature circles are student-centered book discussion groups where each student has a role for which he or she is responsible. Using the literature circle concept, teachers can accommodate a wide variety of student reading levels and allow for differentiated instruction. The use of roles in the literature circle promotes reading, writing, and listening skills, and allows for individual student assessment. Literature circles have become a popular reading comprehension tool in many schools. Research has found literature circles to be successful as an education tool for reading literature as well as content area reading. The collaborative aspects of literature circles support students working with others in an engaging and lower-risk environment. Some of the key ideas supporting the concepts developed in literature circles were described in the results from the National Reading Research Center's five-year study program concerning literacy instruction. Their findings indicate that students should experience these kinds of opportunities because (Baumann and Duffy 8):

- thinking and talking about books promote students' critical understanding of the reading material

- discussions about books in peer groups or among students across grade levels enhance students' involvement, interest, and learning

A recent National Reading Panel Report discussed the motivational effect of computers and stated that the "rapid development of capabilities of computer technology, particularly in speech recognition and multimedia presentations, promises even more successful applications in literacy for the future" (6-9). The report also discussed positive applications of word processing, multimedia software, and hypertext toward reading instructional tasks (U.S. Department of Health and Human Services 2000). Using technology tools as an educational scaffolding strategy can assist students in their learning and moving to higher-level tasks.

The purpose of this book is to provide information and instruction on how to expand and enhance the role-based literature circle with technology. Computer and Internet technologies can assist today's students in reading and comprehension. The book is divided into six chapters that lead the reader from understanding today's students and literature circle concepts to familiarity with ways to use technology to enhance the effectiveness of the literature circle, such as using electronic forms of texts, technology-based activities or roles, and distance learning. In Chapter 1 the new student generation, the millennials, are discussed along with how our definition of literacy has been changing. Chapter 2 describes the literature circle concept and provides nontechnology role sheets for a circle activity. Chapter 3 introduces the technology applications for literature circles, with applications of using electronic forms of text, or eBooks, as the reading material for a literature circle, along with Web sites where eBooks can be obtained. Chapter 4 introduces technology-enhanced roles for literature circle activities. These technology-integrated roles require students to use digital applications of search and research, multimedia, and technology for organization. Chapter 5 is about resources and applications of the online environment concerning logs, journaling, and discussions. The final chapter describes and provides resources for how literature circle activities can be used in distance-learning situations. Each chapter also describes some technology management and educator collaboration ideas.

At the top of Chapters 2 through 6 is a list of student standards related to the content of that chapter. These standards come from the American Association of School Librarians (AASL) Information Literacy Standards and the International Society for Technology in Education (ISTE) Technology Foundation Standards for All Students. The activities and instructional strategies presented in each of these chapters, when implemented with students, can help them achieve the associated standards.

AASL Information Literacy Standards

Information Literacy

1. The student who is information literate accesses information efficiently and effectively.

2. The student who is information literate evaluates information critically and competently.

3. The student who is information literate uses information accurately and creatively.

Independent Learning

4. The student who is an independent learner is information literate and pursues information related to personal interests.

5. The student who is an independent learner is information literate and appreciates literature and other creative expressions of information.

6. The student who is an independent learner is information literate and strives for excellence in information seeking and knowledge generation.

Social Responsibility

7. The student who contributes positively to the learning community and to society is information literate and recognizes the importance of information to a democratic society.

8. The student who contributes positively to the learning community and to society is information literate and practices ethical behavior in regard to information and information technology.

9. The student who contributes positively to the learning community and to society is information literate and participates effectively in groups to pursue and generate information (AASL 1998).

ISTE Technology Foundation Standards for All Students

1. Basic operations and concepts
    1.1. Students demonstrate a sound understanding of the nature and operation of technology systems.
    1.2. Students are proficient in the use of technology.

2. Social, ethical, and human issues
    2.1. Students understand the ethical, cultural, and societal issues related to technology.
    2.2. Students practice responsible use of technology systems, information, and software.
    2.3. Students develop positive attitudes toward technology uses that support lifelong learning, collaboration, personal pursuits, and productivity.

3. Technology productivity tools
    3.1. Students use technology tools to enhance learning, increase productivity, and promote creativity.
    3.2. Students use productivity tools to collaborate in constructing technology-enhanced models, prepare publications, and produce other creative works.

4. Technology communications tools
    4.1. Students use telecommunications to collaborate, publish, and interact with peers, experts, and other audiences.
    4.2. Students use a variety of media and formats to communicate information and ideas effectively to multiple audiences.

5. Technology research tools
    5.2. Students use technology to locate, evaluate, and collect information from a variety of sources.
    5.2. Students use technology tools to process data and report results.
    5.3. Students evaluate and select new information resources and technological innovations based on the appropriateness for specific tasks.

6. Technology problem-solving and decision-making tools
    6.1. Students use technology resources for solving problems and making informed decisions.
    6.2. Students employ technology in the development of strategies for solving problems in the real world (ISTE 2000).

References

AASL (American Association of School Librarians). "Information Literacy Standards for Student Learning: Standards and Indicators." *American Association of School Librarians and Association for Educational Communications and Technology* (1998). Retrieved October 2005 from <http://www.ala.org/ala/aasl/aaslproftools/informationpower/InformationLiteracyStandards_final.pdf>.

Baumann, J. F. and A. M. Duffy. "Engaged Reading for Pleasure and Learning: A Report from the National Reading Research Center." Athens, GA: NRRC (1997). Electronic version ERIC document ED413579 retrieved from <http://eric.ed.gov/ERICDocs/data/ericdocs2/content_storage_01/0000000b/80/23/2c/bc.pdf>.

ISTE (International Society for Technology in Education "Technology Foundation Standards for All Students." ISTE National Educational Technology Standards for Students (NETS*S) (2000). Retrieved October 2005 from <http://cnets.iste.org/students/s_stands.html>.

U.S. Department of Health and Human Services. "Chapter 6: Computer Technology and Reading." Instruction Reports of the Subgroups Report of the National Reading Panel: *Teaching Children to Read* (2000). Retrieved September 2004 from <http://www.nichd.nih.gov/publications/nrp/report.htm>.

Chapter 1

Today's Technology-Enhanced Student

Digital Age

As we move more into the information era, the way we look at things and how things look are changing. In today's information-based society technology is all around us, and this technological world is one where our students of today are living. In a recent U.S. Census report, there are now more homes in the U.S. with computers than homes without them (U.S. Census 2000), numbers which have only been increasing since the census. Today's schools have access to technology; most schools have some form of computer access for students. An evaluation done on secondary schools found that by 2001 at least 78% of secondary schools had made computers available to students outside the regular school day (U.S. DOE 2002).

Today's students are a group to whom the Internet and other forms of communication technology stimulate interest in learning in general and an interest in researching and innovating using technology. Using a technology-integrated approach with the literature circle should help today's teachers with their technology-focused students as they engage in reading activities. Today's students, sometimes called *millenials* or the *millennial generation,* are people who have grown and come of age along with the Internet. It has always been there for them; they see the Internet as something that has always been available to them, with free and ubiquitous information that they can access at any time. They prefer to find information using the Internet, because they feel that the information is more abundant, accessible, and up-to-date (U.S. DOE 2004).

Susan Patrick, Director of Educational Technology for the U.S. Department of Education, describes the technological world of the millenials as being quite different from any before (see Figure 1.1). This population of nearly 50 million students in our schools represents the largest and most diverse group in our educational history. Some of the elements of this new information-age student include (Patrick, 2004):

- 28% of high school students access foreign news sources via the Internet
- 90% of children between ages 5 and 17 use computers
- Teens spend more time online using the Internet than watching television
- 94% of online teens use the Internet for school-related research
- 72% of first graders used a home computer during the summer on a weekly basis
- Over 85% of young children with home computers use them for educational purposes
- 97% of kindergartners in 1999 had access to a computer at school or home
- 35% of two- to five-year-old children use the Internet
- 71% of online teens indicate they rely on Internet sources for projects
- 48% of teens think that the Internet improves their relationships
- 94% of online teens report using the Internet for school-related research
- 74% of online teens use instant messaging
- 24% of online teens have created their own Web pages or sites
- 43% of children (4-18) in 2003 owned at least one wireless device (up over 10% in one year)
- 13% of children age 7 and under own a wireless device

Patrick further explains how even today's schools are different. Citing 1994-2002 U.S. Statistics from NCES, she describes some of the technological conditions of today's schools (Patrick 2004):

- 99% of schools are connected to the Internet
- 94% of schools have broadband
- 92% of instructional rooms have Internet access

Figure 1.1 Internet use by age.

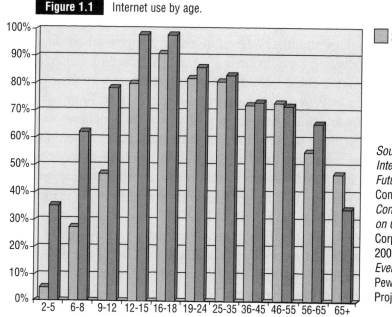

2000   2002

Source: Cole, Jeffrey I., et al. *UCLA Internet Report: Surveying the Digital Future, Year Three.* UCLA Center for Communication Policy. Feb. 2003; *Connected to the Future: A Report on Children's Internet Use.* Corporation for Public Broadcasting. 2002; Horrigan, John, et al. *The Ever-Shifting Internet Population.* Pew Internet & American Life Project. 16 Apr. 2003.

- 23% of public schools use wireless networks
- 8% of public schools lent laptops to students
- Schools on average have a 5:1 student to computer ratio

Today's students live in a world filled with new types of information, communication, presentation, and publication systems. At the same time, these technologies are giving wide access to information with technologies that will also support ways of managing, analyzing, developing, and monitoring information. Many of today's students are already familiar with these technology capabilities, while others are not. In contrast, many of today's teachers are not technologically literate (at least not to their students' levels). Schools may have limited or unreliable technological capacity and most educational systems are not adequately preparing students to develop the types and levels of literacy necessary to capitalize upon technology-enhanced teaching and learning. Even schools that have success at fostering high literacy for their students often don't include digital technologies such as hypertext, technology-based reading and writing, and other forms of technology integration. The school is becoming very different from the outside world, as most school students and adult professionals use these valuable, technology-based communication and research tools on a daily basis outside the classroom (Meltzer, J., Smith, N. C. and Clark, H. 2001). We must remember that we are not educating our students for the past, but instead for their present and future as part of our information-age society. Integrating Internet and computer applications into methods such as the literature circle will provide direction and effective integration of technology for student success.

New Literacies

Traditionally, literacy focused on the ability to read words on paper including books, newspapers, and job applications. Congress, with the 1991 National Literacy Act, defined literacy as "an individual's ability to read, write, and speak in English, and compute and solve problems at levels of proficiency necessary to function on the job and in society, to achieve one's goals, and develop one's knowledge and potential" (NIFL 1991 "What is the NALS?").

The concept of literacy in today's world is changing. This new concept of literacy goes beyond only paper to include reading from computer screens and personal devices to include media, technology, information, and other critical literacies (Semali 2001). The Internet and other forms of information and communication technology (ICT) such as word processors, Web editors, presentation software, and e-mail are regularly redefining the nature of literacy. In order for a student to become fully literate in today's world, he or she must become proficient in the new literacies of ICT. Educators should integrate these technologies into today's literacy curriculum in order to prepare students for their literacy future. The International Reading Association (IRA) believes that much can be done to support students in developing the new literacies that will be required in their future. IRA (2002) states that students have the right to:

- have teachers who are skilled and effective at using new literacies for teaching and learning

- a literacy curriculum that integrates these new literacies into the instructional program
- instruction that develops these literacies for effective use
- assessment practices in literacy that include electronic reading and writing
- opportunities to learn safe and responsible use of information and communication technologies
- equal access to information and communication technology

Literacy and Technology

With today's computer and Internet technologies, educators have tools with features valuable for learners with various abilities, language backgrounds, and special needs. The unique features and capabilities of these technologies can provide interactions that many students need to be successful with text-based materials. The availability of electronic text, Internet access, and access to computer software in many forms is increasing, making it easier for educators to integrate technology into education. As Jeff Wilhelm (2000) states in his writing, concerning literacy and technology, for today's students "technology has everything to do with literacy ... electronic technologies has everything to do with being literate" (4). Educators need to consider the options of integrating the technology as a basic part of what students do for class, using the technology's abilities and functions, creating high-interest activities while at the same time providing additional supports or accommodations. Using today's desktop, laptop, or handheld computers with software, educators can integrate information technology into the literature circle and create activities that are individually tailored to the reader in a cooperative group, and increase the reader's interactivity with the text itself. These features and capabilities of technologies can provide the interest and scaffolding that many students need to be successful with text-based materials.

Research has found that most Internet-using students say their teachers don't make good use of the Web as a classroom tool. According to the study commissioned by the Pew Internet and American Life Project, *The Digital Disconnect: The Widening Gap Between Internet-Savvy Students and Their Schools*, many schools and teachers have not yet recognized the new ways students communicate and access information over the Internet. Students feel a disconnect between how they use the Internet and how it is used in schools, with many feeling that the assignments given at school actually discourage them from using the Internet as much, or as creatively, as they would like (Levin and Arafeh 2002). This author's interviews of teachers and their experiences revealed that teachers' educational experiences often do not include technology integration in education. In addition, many support text material do not include integrated technology. For example, in an analysis of a commonly used book on the literature circle, a search through the book found that the words technology, Internet, and eBook do not appear in 176 pages of the text, and that the word computer is used just once in the entire book. The problem for many of our teachers is a disconnect between the subject material and their experience with technology integration. They teach in a digital age but have not received a digitally integrated education. The purpose of this book is to assist teachers and students in integrating technology into an effective reading instructional strategy, the literature circle.

Figure 1.2 Dimensions of using technology in the literature circle.

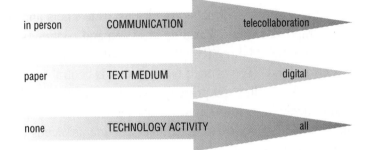

Technology-Enhanced Literature Circle

in person	COMMUNICATION	telecollaboration
paper	TEXT MEDIUM	digital
none	TECHNOLOGY ACTIVITY	all

Integrating Technology

The integration of the literature circle with educational technologies can be implemented into the wide variety of today's classrooms, from fully face-to-face to fully online (see Figure 1.2). In some of the learning circle activities, the teacher and students can interact with each other in an online environment. This provides teachers and students with experience using technology-enhanced activities for distance learning or with hospital or homebound students. It is important to prepare our students to be able to interact with each other using methods that students can and want to use. The technology-enhanced literature circle is one such way.

Teachers can integrate technology into the literature circle along any or all of three facets: communication between students; the text material itself; and student activities. The range for communication goes from members participating in person in class, to students who participate through telecommunications, perhaps as hospital or homebound students, to interactions through telecommunications between the in-person class and different classes or grade levels, to a distance-learning situation in which all students communicate through telecommunications. The text material used for the literature circle can range from paper-based text, to paper-based text with digital enhancements or versions, to fully digital text, such as eBooks. For the activities, students can participate using just paper and pencil to using technologies such as search engines, paint programs, concept mapping software or Web sites, digital recording, and chat software. These activities can range from no technology integration, to partial integration such as a one-computer classroom in which students take turns, to complete integration in which students have one-to-one computer access.

Integrating technology into literature circles helps students meet content standards in reading, literacy, and language arts and also helps them achieve technology standards. Using a thoughtfully designed technology-enhanced literature circle approach, students can have experiences in all six Technology Foundation Standards for All Students from the ISTE National Educational Technology Standards (NETS) (ISTE 2000):

- Basic operations and concepts
- Social, ethical, and human issues
- Technology productivity tools

- Technology communications tools
- Technology research tools
- Technology problem-solving and decision-making tools

The variety of book formats provides us, as teachers and students, tools by which we can improve reading. Reading has been and continues to be a basic part of education, from the old three R's (Reading, 'Riting, and 'Rithmatic) to today's "No Child Left Behind." The printed word or text is central to our culture, and many teachers make reading the primary focus of education. Using technology, such as digital media including electronic text, teachers can surpass the traditional forms with technology's ability to meet diverse students' needs (Meyer and Rose 2002). Barton (2000) estimates that the average literacy required for all American occupations should rise by about 14% over a ten-year period. While reading may remain constant, how we teach reading and the tools that we use may change.

While technology as a tool for education exists, today there are still reading problems with students. These reading difficulties make educators, schools, and students frustrated. It is estimated, from a national longitudinal study, that more than 17% of young children will encounter a problem learning to read (NCITE 1996). Additionally, the National Assessment of Education Progress (NAEP) report indicated that in 1994 all schools in the U.S. have a number of children who are failing the task of learning to read. In the report it was found that 8.7 million 4th- through 12th-graders read below grade level, with 42% of 4th-graders, 31% of 8th-graders and 30% of 12th-graders reading at a "below basic" level (NAEP 2001). The literacy gap is even larger when focused on minority students, students with learning disabilities, and students whose first language is not English (ELL, ESOL, ESL). As an example, approximately half of the African-American and Hispanic 8th-grade students read below the basic level (Black 2005).

Educational professionals and other stakeholders increasingly voice support for inclusion of technology in a literacy program, because technology plays an increasingly central role in our society (Biancarosa and Snow 2004). Technology can be both a facilitator of literacy and a medium of literacy. Teachers and students should use technology applications as both instructional tools and instructional topics. Technology tools can assist teachers by providing needed supports for struggling readers, through methods such as instructional reinforcement and guided practice. As a topic by itself, technology is changing the reading and writing demands of today's student and of society.

To help students with reading fluency, teachers need to provide activities and instruction to students. To achieve this goal for reading, teachers can assist students by increasing practice through audiotapes and other technologies (NIFL 2002). Using eBooks or other technologies in a literature circle is an excellent application to achieve this goal. University of Georgia's Donna Alvermann reports that "students of the Net Generation [millenials] are quick to find Internet sites and understand complex materials ... these children, who scored in the lowest 25 percentile on a standardized reading test, can read some materials when they are motivated to do so" (Alvermann 2002 Response to John Guthrie by Donna Alvermann).

The technology integrations or enhancements described in this book apply the technology tools that are commonly available on a typical computer with Internet access. They can be applied to classes that meet in person and also to classes or students that interact in an online environment. Some of the specific role assignments described will use various kinds of technology applications such as search engines and specific Web sites to do research. Other role assignments will have students using programs to make drawings, record their voices, and make concept maps. Classes can also use digital forms of books while in their literature circle and for other activities. Each of these topics will be expanded in later chapters.

References

Alvermann, Donna. "Adolescent Literacy – Research Informing Practice: A Series of Workshops" [Electronic Version]. The Partnership for Reading (n.d.). Retrieved April 2005 from <http://www.nifl.gov/partnershipforreading/adolescent/summary.html>.

Barton, Paul E. "What Jobs Require: Literacy, Education, and Training, 1940-2006" [Electronic Version].Washington, DC: Educational Testing Service (2000). Retrieved April 2005 from <http://www.ets.org/media/research/pdf/picjobs.pdf>.

Biancarosa, Gina and Catherine E. Snow. "Reading Next: A Vision for Action and Research in Middle and High School Literacy" [Electronic Version]. Alliance for Excellent Education (2004). Retrieved April 2005 from <http://www.all4ed.org/publications/ReadingNext/ReadingNext.pdf>.

Black, S. "Reaching the Older Reader" [Electronic Version]. *American School Board Journal*. National School Boards Association. Retrieved April 2005 from <http://www.asbj.com/current/research.html>.

IRA (International Reading Association). (2002) (*Integrating Literacy and Technology in the Curriculum: A Position Statemen*). Newark, Delaware.

ISTE (International Society for Technology in Education). "National Educational Technology Standards for Students: Technology Foundation Standards for All Students." *International Society for Technology in Education* (2000). Retrieved August 2005, from <http://cnets.iste.org/students/s_stands.html>.

Levin, Douglas and Sousan Arafeh. *The Digital Disconnect: The Widening Gap Between Internet-Savvy Students and Their Schools*. Pew Internet and American Life Project (2002). Retrieved October 2004 from <http://www.pewInternet.org/pdfs/PIP_Schools_Internet_Report.pdf>.

Meltzer, Julie, Nancy Cook Smith, and Holly Clark. "Adolescent Literacy Resources: Linking Research and Practice" [Electronic Version]. LAB at Brown University (2001). Retrieved April 2005 from <http://www.alliance.brown.edu/pubs/adlit/alr_lrp.pdf>.

Meyer, Anne and David H. Rose. *Learning to Read in the Computer Age* [Electronic Version]. Brookline Books, 1999. Retrieved November 2004 from <http://www.cast.org/publications/book/ltr/index.html>.

National Assessment of Education Progress (NAEP). *NAEP Achievement Levels for Reading 1992-1998* (2001). Available online at <http://www.nagb.org/pubs/readingbook.pdf>.

National Center to Improve the Tools of Educators (NCITE). *Learning to Read/Reading to Learn Campaign; Helping Children with Learning Disabilities to Succeed* [Electronic Version] (1996). Available online at <http://idea.uoregon.edu/~ncite/programs/read.html>.

National Institute for Literacy (NIFL). *Put Reading First: The Research Building Blocks for Teaching Children to Read* (2002). Available online at <http://www.nifl.gov>.

Patrick, Susan. *e-Learning and Students Today: Options for No Child Left Behind.* Speech presented at the No Child Left Behind Summit. Orlando, FL, July 2004.

Semali, L. (2001, November). *Defining New Literacies in Curricular Practice* [Electronic Version]. Reading Online, (5)4. Retrieved October, 2004, from <http://www.readingonline.org/newliteracies/lit_index.asp?HREF=semali1/index.html>.

U.S. Department of Education (U.S. DOE), Office of Educational Technology (OET). *Toward A New Golden Age in American Education: How the Internet, the Law and Today's Students Are Revolutionizing Expectations* [Electronic Version]. Washington, DC, 2004. Retrieved April 2005 from <http://www.ed.gov/about/offices/list/os/technology/plan/2004/plan.pdf>.

U.S. Department of Education, National Center for Education Statistics. *Internet Access in U.S. Public Schools and Classrooms: 1994-2001* (2002). NCES 2002-018, by Anne Kleiner and Elizabeth Farris. Project Officer: Bernard Greene. Washington, DC.

Wilhelm, J. (2002). *Literacy by Design: Why is All This Technology So Important?* Voices in the Middle, 7(3), 4-6.

The Literature Circle

The American Association of School Librarians (AASL)
Information Literacy Standards addressed in this chapter:

- Information Literacy: 1 and 3
- Independent Learning: 4, 5, and 6
- Social Responsibility: 7, 8, and 9

For more information on these standards, see page ix.

What Is a Literature Circle?

For most of the education community, the literature circle was first introduced in 1994 though Harvey Daniels's book, *Literature Circles: Voice and Choice in Book Clubs and Reading Groups*. Literature circles are known by many different names including literature studies, literacy circles, book clubs, literature discussion groups, literature study groups, and cooperative book discussion groups. All literature circles share the three basic elements: diversity, self-choice, and student initiative (Daniels, 2002). According to Schlick, Noe, and Johnson (1999), a literature circle is more than a book club. Where a book club's discussion only centers on events and plot, a literature circle format promotes discussion from varying perspectives, which provides members with a deeper understanding of the text. Literature circles occur as students, who are reading the same story, article, book, or other text, join together in small groups to discuss the material being read. Students will read a determined portion of the text, either in class or outside of class, and then each member of the discussion group takes specific responsibilities, or roles, in the discussion, so that everyone comes to the group with the notes or material needed to perform their assigned role. These literature-circle discussion groups should have regular meetings, with the discussion roles changing periodically. Ideally, as students become proficient in analyzing the reading material with their discussion group, specific roles would not need to be assigned, as students become engaged in a more open-ended discussion of their reading.

In a standard literature circle, student activities would be on the far left of the technology-enhanced continuum, where students interact in person, using a printed on paper book, and usually not having any technology-based activities to work with concerning their interactions with the text and other students (see Figure 2.1).

Figure 2.1 Dimensions of using technology in the literature circle.

Technology-Enhanced Literature Circle

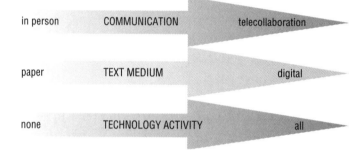

in person	COMMUNICATION	telecollaboration
paper	TEXT MEDIUM	digital
none	TECHNOLOGY ACTIVITY	all

Literature Circle Design and Benefits

The literature circle is a student-centered, cooperative-learning reading activity for a group of four to six students at any grade level or subject area. The collaborative elements of literature circles assist in creating a student-centered learning environment. As students interact in structured discussion and extended responses, in a variety of learning and intelligence styles, students are guided to a deeper understanding of their reading. In a role-based literature circle, each member of a circle is assigned a specific role, with specific responsibilities, which are used to guide the group in a discussion of the text material they are all reading. Literature circles provide a way for students to engage in critical thinking and reflection as they read, discuss, and respond to books, articles, stories, or other reading material. The literature circle assignments, or roles, guide students to a deeper understanding of what they read through structured discussion and extended written and artistic response. Literature circles provide a constructive educational opportunity for students to control their own learning as they share thoughts, concerns, and their understanding of the concepts, events, and material presented in what is being read. The benefits of literature circles include (Day et. al. 2002):

■ Scaffolding to teach and not merely check comprehension

■ Allowing teachers to provide instruction to many facets of comprehension

■ Encouraging students to learn from one another

- Motivating students naturally
- Promoting discussion more effectively than whole groups

A goal of literature circles is to scaffold, assist, and guide students to become more independent and competent with text discussions and strategies for understanding through teacher coaching (MCPS 2000). Based upon the curriculum goal or topics being studied, the teacher selects a set of texts, which can be topic or thematically related books, or works by a single author (Brabham and Villaume 2000). The literature circle allows students to master content, genre, and other aspects of what they read through a formalized discussion process. Each student is assigned a role connected to a different strength or focus. The literature circle has proved especially successful in getting all students to participate in a discussion through asking questions and responding to each other. Through the use of a variety of roles, literature circles allow students with particular strengths or learning styles to employ them to analyze the reading material (literature), while at the same time provide students opportunities to explore different styles of understanding text within the small-group setting.

In their report *Reading Next: A Vision for Action and Research in Middle and High School Literacy,* from the Carnegie Corporation, Biancarosa and Snow (2004) recommend fifteen key elements of effective adolescent literacy programs as classroom-based strategies to improve adolescent literacy; at least seven of those fifteen elements can be applied to the literature circle:

1. **Direct, explicit comprehension instruction.** Instruction should be concerned with comprehension strategies and processes for readers to use in understanding their reading. Strategies include modeling, scaffolding, summarizing, metacognition, and discussing texts with others.

2. **Effective instructional principles embedded in content.** Reading should include language arts teachers embedding instruction using content-area texts. Content-area teachers should provide instruction specific to their subject area while at the same time reinforcing reading and writing skills and strategies.

3. **Motivation and self-directed learning.** Students need to become more engaged in their reading, such as by participating in reading-related choices. Material should also be available that has relevancy to students' lives.

4. **Text-based collaborative learning.** Students interact in activities going beyond talking and instead work collaboratively in small groups. In the language arts classroom and other subject-area classes, students of different ability levels or interests use a variety of text materials as part of a literature circle.

5. **Strategic tutoring.** Some students need additional individualized instruction concerning reading strategies, such as with decoding and fluency.

6. **Diverse texts.** Students need access to a variety "diverse texts," at various reading and difficulty levels representing a wide variety of topics.

7. **A technology component.** Use technology as a tool and a medium for literacy instruction. Technology can be used to provide reading supports and scaffolds as well as used as a reading topic.

A five-year study conducted by Dr. Judith A. Langer, Director of the National Research Center on English Learning & Achievement, found six interrelated and supporting features for effective instruction concerning reading and writing (Langer, J. E., Close, J. Angelis, and P. Preller 2000). Of these six features, four relate directly to how students can participate in a role-based literature circle (3):

1. Students learn skills and knowledge in multiple lesson types.

4. Students learn strategies for doing the work.

5. Students are expected to be generative thinkers.

6. Classrooms foster cognitive collaboration.

Concerning literacy instruction and classroom design, literature circles are a method for students to share reading experiences. Integrating the Internet into the classroom can extend the literature circle by providing a worldwide audience for sharing, along with resources for better understanding the literature and using the technology tools to assist students in accessing, organizing, analyzing, and communicating their approaches to essential questions (Lamb, Smith, and Johnson1999).

Role Sheet Rationale

Some teachers use role sheets with their students during a literature circle, but others find that the roles may take focus and energy away from the discussion. While many consider that the goal of a teacher is to move beyond the use of assignment or role sheets, others, especially those new, either teachers or students, may prefer the use of role sheets as job aids. An advantage of the role sheets is that the sheets themselves can be used for accountability and assessment purposes, providing physical documentation of student work and ability. Role sheets can also provide needed direction and assistance to students with special needs, many of whom might otherwise find a discussion a difficult or taxing activity.

A set of role sheets for a non-technology-based literature circle activity is included at the end of this chapter.

The Teacher's Role in the Literature Circle

Students are not the only ones with roles to play in the literature circle; teachers have their own role to play. It is important for teachers to provide direction and facilitation to the discussion groups. During each literature circle event, teachers should:

1. Assist students in joining literature circles (discussion groups).

2. Assign roles for the members of each circle.

3. Assign reading to be completed by the circles inside or outside of class.

4. Select circle meeting days – daily, weekly, biweekly, for example.

5. Meet with each group, or mingle among the groups, to check on their progress and help keep students on task.

6. Help students prepare for their roles in their circle; for example, have students read their role descriptions aloud without giving answers.

7. Act as a facilitator for the circles, for example, teachers can ask students to summarize the reading or discuss aspects of their roles.

8. Assess the student work.

Educator Collaboration

Teachers and library media specialists can collaborate in developing literature circle activities. Library media specialists can work with a teacher to identify high-interest reading topics and texts. They can come into classes to provide instruction concerning effective library research strategies along with ethical research behaviors.

Library media specialists can assist teachers by assembling book collections and classroom book sets. They can promote the literature circle topics in the library media center by creating associated displays. Library media specialists can organize space within the library media center, creating centers associated with the literature circle discussion by displaying other books on the same topics, as well as more books by the chosen authors. Most library media specialists also create a Web presence. Working with classroom instructors, the library media specialist can develop a school Web page to direct students to additional online resources concerning the topics or associated versions of the texts in electronic format.

Basic Literature Circle Model

1. Obtain four to five (or more) copies of a number of different books. Make sure that the books have some variation in reading level: easy, average, and challenging.

2. Set the books or book descriptions out for students to review.

3. Students list their preferences for which book group they wish to join. They can use an index card to number their preferences in order. The teacher compiles the cards and uses his or her understanding of the students' reading levels and choices to assign students into groups. Most educators prefer heterogeneous groups for this type of activity.

4. Student groups can now meet and do a pre-reading activity, such as complete a KWL (Know-Want-Learned concept map) about the book. Students can also now make a response or reading journal in which to write their findings from each role they assume and other thoughts, ideas, or questions that they develop while reading.

5. Students can read their books alone, with a partner or reading buddy, or in small groups. Readings can be set by chapter, or number of pages (it is usually better to have small daily goals rather than large weekly goals for student readings). One helpful strategy is to have the group start by having a single member or a few group members read aloud for the first and maybe second

chapters, depending on length. The group can then practice their reading strategies and discuss developments, questions, ideas, and word meanings as they occur. After the initial meeting, the teacher or group leader can assign the next pages to read for homework. Teachers might wish to have students meet daily for a few minutes to check on each other's readings and remind the students about what reading homework pages are to be read next.

6. As students read, they should somehow flag in their books important elements, questions, or discussion points with sticky notes (paper or digital), or write in response journals. Paper sticky notes can be easily transferred into reading journals.

7. During the full literature circle meeting, students will complete their roles and associated job aids or worksheets. These roles may be assigned to an individual for a few days or for a week. Students should experience a variety of role assignments throughout a reading project by rotating roles until they finish their book.

8. When they have finished their literature circle book and discussion, students should complete some form of self or group evaluation.

The Literature Circle in the Inclusion Setting

The inclusion model, in which a special needs student participates in the "regular" classroom, has become the current classroom education standard. Of the nearly 46 million students enrolled in grades K-12 in U.S. public schools during the 2000-2001 school year, approximately 11.5 percent, or 5.5 million students, were classified as having some kind of disability (Koenig and Bachman 2004). In addition, over 10%, or five million students, were identified as English as a second language learners (ELL, ESOL, ESL, LEP) (NCELA 2004). Today, students with special needs have an increasing impact on all teachers as, during the past ten years, the percentage of students with disabilities served in schools and classes with their nondisabled peers has gradually grown. In the U.S. for the 1999-2000 school year, the number of students with disabilities served was 588,300 preschool children and 5,683,707 students ages 6 through 21, an increase of 2.6% over the previous year (U.S. DOE 2002). For example, during the 1997-98 school year, U.S. states reported that 94.7 percent of students ages 12 through 17 with disabilities were served in schools with their nondisabled peers (see Figure 2.2) (U.S. DOE 2000; U.S. DOE 1996). How does this affect the classroom and the literature circle? In summarizing research Meltzer, Smith, and Clark (2001) state that the following combination of literacy practices will result in enhanced literacy for diverse learners:

1. Teacher strategies taught and used in context rather than in isolation.

2. A focus on reading and writing.

3. The importance of speaking and listening, with frequent opportunities to collaboratively brainstorm, organize, write, read, share, revise, and present

4. An emphasis on thinking, combining cognitive and metacognitive strategies to enhance learning.

5. The establishment of student-centered classrooms.

Each of these strategies can be applied with a literature circle and can assist all students.

Figure 2.2 Percentage of Students Age 6 through 21 in Different Education Environments during 1988-89 through 1997-98.

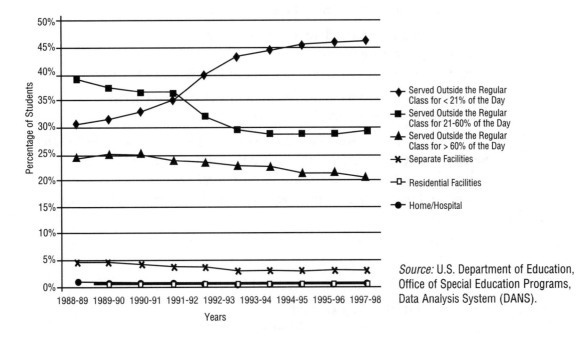

Source: U.S. Department of Education, Office of Special Education Programs, Data Analysis System (DANS).

Literature Circles and Differentiated Instruction

Using a literature circle approach allows teachers to use a differentiated instruction model that recognizes that students have different background knowledge, readiness, language, learning styles, and interests. Differentiated instruction is an educational approach to teaching and learning for students of differing abilities in the same class, with the intent to maximize growth and success while assisting in the learning process (Hall n.d.)

According to Willis and Mann (2000) in summarizing the research of Tomlinson on differentiated instruction, teachers can differentiate three aspects of the curriculum: content, process, and products. *Content* refers to the concepts, principles, and skills that students are to learn and the strategies teachers use to provide students access to those skills and knowledge. *Process* refers to the activities that students participate in where flexible grouping is used; these activities can be modified or provided with more scaffolding, depending on a student's readiness. *Products* refers to projects and materials that are created that demonstrate what students have learned; different students can create different products based on their own readiness levels, interests, and learning style. Each of these three aspects can be related to the roles within a literature circle.

The educational needs of the students in any classroom today vary considerably, as do the strategies for meeting them. One strategy that teachers can use in today's inclusive classroom is the literature circle.

Web Resources

The Literature Circles Resource Center
<http://www.litcircles.org/>

Laura Candler's Literature Circle Site
<http://home.att.net/~teaching/litcircles.htm>

Office of Educational Research and Improvement (U.S.)
Article on Literature Circles
<http://www.homeedsa.com/Articles/Literature%20Circles.asp>

Elementary school teacher's experiences of Literature Circles
<http://teachers.net/gazette/MAR02/zeiger.html>

Article from *Education World* on the Use of Literature Circles in School Settings "Literature Circles Build Excitement for Books!"
<http://www.education-world.com/a_curr/curr259.shtml>
Advice and useful links in this motivating article found on *Education World*.

Book Discussion Guides

Beacon Press Reading Guides
<http://www.beacon.org/client/readguide/>

BookBrowse.com Reading Guides
<http://www.bookbrowse.com/reading_guides/>

HarperCollins Reading Group Guides
<http://www.harpercollins.com/readers.asp>

Henry Holt and Company Reading Guides
<http://www.henryholt.com/readingguides/index.htm>

Kids Reads
<http://www.kidsreads.com/clubs/index.asp>

Multnomah County Library
<http://www.multcolib.org/books/bookgroups>

Teen Reads
<http://www.teenreads.com/clubs/index.asp>

Paul Brians' Study Guides
<http://www.wsu.edu:8080/~brians/guides_index.html>

Penguin Books Reading Group Guides
<http://www.penguinputnam.com/static/html/readingguides/index.html>

Random House Reading Group Guides
<http://www.randomhouse.com/reader_resources/browsetitle/>

Reading Group Guides
<http://www.readinggroupguides.com/>

References

Biancarosa, Gina and Catherine E. Snow. "Reading Next: A Vision for Action and Research in Middle and High School Literacy." *Alliance for Excellent Education* (2004). Retrieved April 2004 from <http://www.all4ed.org/publications/ReadingNext/ReadingNext.pdf>.

Brabham, E.G., and S. K. Villaume. "Questions and answers: Continuing conversations about literature circles." *The Reading Teacher* (2000), 54(3), 278-280.

Daniels, Harvey. *Literature Circles: Voice and Choice in the Student-Centered Classrooms.* York, ME: Stenhouse Publishers (1994).

Daniels, Harvey. *Literature circles: Voice and choice in book clubs and reading groups.* (2nd ed.). Portland, ME: Stenhouse Publishers (2002).

Day, Jeni Pollack, Dixie Lee Spiegle, Janet McLellan, and Valerie B. Brown. *Moving Forward With Literature Circles: How to Plan, Manage, and Evaluate Literature Circles That Deepen Understanding and Foster a Love of Reading (Theory and practice).* New York, NY: Scholastic Professional Books (2002).

Hall, Tracey. "Differentiated Instruction." *Center for Applied Special Technology* (CAST) (n.d.). Retrieved May 2005 from <http://www.cast.org/publications/ncac/ncac_diffinstruc.html>.

Koenig, Judith Andersion and Lyle F. Bachman. *Keeping Score for All: The Effects of Inclusion and Accommodation Policies on Large-Scale Educational Assessment.* Board on Testing and Assessment Center for Education. The National Academies Press. Washington, DC (2004): 1.

Lamb, Annette, Nancy R. Smith, and Larry Johnson. "Themes and Literature Circles." *eduScapes* (1999, updated 02/03). Retrieved September 2004 from <http://eduscapes.com/ladders/themes/literacy.htm>.

Langer, Judith, Elizabeth Close, Janet Angelis, and Paula Preller. "Guidelines for Teaching Middle and High School Students to Read and Write Well: Six Features of Effective Instruction." National Research Center on English Learning & Achievement, (May 2000). Retrieved April 2005 from <http://cela.albany.edu/publication/brochure/guidelines.pdf>.

MCPS (Montgomery County Public Schools). (2000). Discussion Groups & Literature Circles in the MCPS Early Literacy Guide [Electronic Version]. Retrieved September, 2004, from <http://www.mcps.k12.md.us/curriculum/english/elg_lit_circles.htm#purpose>.

Meltzer, Julie, Nancy Cook Smith, and Holly Clark. "Adolescent Literacy Resources: Linking Research and Practice." LAB at Brown University, 2001. Retrieved April 2005 from <http://www.alliance.brown.edu/pubs/adlit/alr_lrp.pdf>.

NCELA (National Clearinghouse for English Language Acquisition and Language Instructional Programs). 2002-2003 NCELA Poster. *National Clearinghouse for English Language Acquisition and Language Instructional Programs* (2004). Retrieved April 2005 from <http://www.ncela.gwu.edu/policy/states/reports/statedata/2002LEP/Growing_LEP0203.pdf>.

Schlick Noe, K. L. and Johnson, N.J. (1999). *Getting Started with Literature Circles.* Christopher-Gordon Publishers, Inc.

Willis, Scott, and Larry Mann. *Differentiating Instruction: Finding Manageable Ways to Meet Individual Needs. Curriculum Update* (2000). Retrieved May 2005 from <http://www.ascd.org/ed_topics/cu2000win_willis.html>.

U.S. Department of Education (US DOE). *To assure the free appropriate public education of all children with disabilities. Eighteenth annual report to Congress on the implementation of IDEA.* Washington, DC: author. (1996). Retrieved October 2002 from <http://www.ed.gov/pubs/OSEP96AnlRpt/>.

U.S. Department of Education (US DOE). *To assure the free appropriate public education of all children with disabilities. Twenty-second annual report to Congress on the implementation of IDEA.* Washington, DC: author. (2000). Retrieved October 2002 from <http://www.ed.gov/about/reports/annual/osep/2000/index.html>.

U.S. Department of Education (US DOE). *Twenty-third Annual Report to Congress on the Implementation of the Individuals with Disabilities Education Act* (2002). Retrieved October 2002 from <http://www.ed.gov/about/reports/annual/osep/2001/index.html>.

Discussion Coordinator

Name: _____   Group: _____

Book: _____

Author: _____

Reading Assignment: page _____ to page_____

Assignment:

Your job is to develop a list of questions that your group might want to discuss about this book, or part of the book. Your task is to help people talk over the big ideas in the reading and share the other members' reactions. Usually the best questions come from your own thoughts, feelings, and concerns that occur as you read. You can list these ideas below during or after your reading. If you want, you may use some of the example questions below to help you develop the topics for your group. Part of your job is also to make sure that each group member contributes to the session.

Possible discussion questions or topics for today:

1. _____

2. _____

3. _____

4. _____

5. _____

Sample Questions:

- What went through your mind while you read this book or passage?
- How did you feel while reading this part of the book?
- How would someone summarize this section?
- What was the main point discussed in this book or section?
- At what point did today's reading remind you of any real-life experiences?
- What questions did you have when you finished this section?
- Did anything in this book or section surprise you?
- Describe one or two of the most important ideas presented in the text.
- Predict some things you think will be talked about next.

Vocabulary Elaborator

Name: _____ Group: _____

Book: _____

Author: _____

Reading Assignment: page _____ to page_____

Assignment:

Your job is to develop a list of words for your group to define in the context of this book, or part of book. Your task is to help define these words from the reading and share them with the other members. The words you select to define should be words that you or other members of your group cannot pronounce, define, or understand in the way they are presented. To find your words:

1. First, point to the unexplained word and then underline or highlight it.

2. Next, read the sentence containing the unexplained word.

   a. If you cannot comprehend the meaning of the word, read the preceding sentence to try to figure out the definition.

   b. If you still don't have a definition for the marked word, read the next sentence after the marked word.

3. Lastly, use a dictionary to check the definition of the word.

Usually dictionaries will have several meanings and it is important to look at each numbered definition and decide which one coincides with the marked word.

Words I have never heard before:
Words whose meaning I don't know:
Words I have seen before, but never used this way:

	Word	Page/Paragraph/Line	Definition
1			
2			
3			
4			
5			

Literary Expositor

Name: _____ Group: _____

Book: _____

Author: _____

Reading Assignment: page _____ to page_____

Assignment:

Your job is to select from the book or passage, by yourself or with help, several favorite or interesting passages. Your task is to select three or four of your favorite parts of the story to share aloud with your group members. As you read and find sections that you like, highlight the paragraphs and record the corresponding page numbers you enjoyed reading and want to hear read aloud. Possible reasons for selection include important, well written, humorous, informative, surprising, controversial, funny, confusing, and thought provoking.

      After the book or section has been read in its entirety by the group, the Literary Expositor will read aloud his or her selected paragraphs as group members identify his selections. During the read-aloud segment, the other group members will listen intently as you read the section and determine what particular aspect of the reading they enjoyed the most. You must find at least three, but no more than five, sentences to "read aloud" to your group.

Page/Paragraph/Line	Reason	Sentence
1		
2		
3		
4		
5		

Graphic Illustrator

Name: _____ Group: _____

Book: _____

Author: _____

Reading Assignment: page _____ to page_____

Assignment:

Your job is to draw two pictures that depict the main idea and feeling in the narrative. Your task is to create illustrations, below or on the back, that show a character's interaction with other characters or story elements. After drawing your picture, label the elements to assist everyone with understanding your drawing. Also, draw pictures that show story or text ideas and then discuss your idea pictures with your group. Once your pictures are finished, write out a description of the character's interaction in complete sentences and standard paragraph form.

Picture 1	Picture 2

Paragraph Descriptions: _____

_____

_____

_____

_____

_____

_____

_____

_____

_____

Graphic Organizer

Name: _____   Group: _____

Book: _____

Author: _____

Reading Assignment: page _____ to page_____

Assignment:

Your job is to create a content or concept map from the reading that helps group members better understand the reading. Create your concept map from the reading with the main idea at the center or top and the related ideas moving out with descriptors connecting verbs. Share the map with the other group members and see if they have any other points or connections to add. You can make any type of concept map you wish, or choose from the list below.

Character Map | Timeline | Character Interaction | Story Line/Plot | Compare & Contrast (Venn)

Background Researcher

Name: _____ Group: _____

Book: _____

Author: _____

Reading Assignment: page _____ to page_____

Assignment:

Your job is to read from the text and identify when and where the writing occurred. Your task is to identify the historical time frame or location and research a topic of your choice related to that time or location. In the text, characters behave in a certain manner, or events are described in a certain way, which reflects a specific period in time or location. This is known as the setting. You should investigate a topic of interest that happened in that specific time period or location of the setting. If the book is not story based, identify a fact from the reading, and research that fact to find something of interest to you. In the list below, identify at least three statements that indicate the historical or locational (or factual) setting. Then research an aspect of that time or location and share your findings with your group members.

Setting Statements:

Page/Paragraph/Line	Year/Location	Sentence
1		
2		
3		

Topic of Interest Research Findings: _____

_____

_____

_____

_____

_____

_____

_____

Reference: _____

_____

Connector

Name: _____ Group: _____

Book: _____

Author: _____

Reading Assignment: page _____ to page_____

Assignment:

Your job is to make connections from the reading to other experiences: to other texts, to yourself, or to any other things you have heard about or seen. Your task is to make statements that explain connections between what you are reading and something you have read in the past, some of your own personal experiences, or anything else in the world (for example, the news, movies, television programs, or people). As you read consider what you are reading and try to make the connections. You can create your own connections or use the examples below. Record the page/location of the sentence you are connecting, then rewrite or summarize the sentence, and then explain about the connection.

Connection starters:

■ This book reminds me of _____ (another text) because…

■ I remember reading another book, _____, that also talked about …

■ This part of the reading reminds me of _____ …

■ I felt like _____ (story character) when I …

■ If this had happened to me, I would have…

■ Something similar happened to me when…

■ The reading relates to my life by…

■ This reading reminds me of a news report I saw on television about …

■ This book reminds me of _____ (a movie) that was about …

Connections:

Page	Sentence	Connection
1		
2		
3		

Mapper/Tracker

Name: _____   Group: _____

Book: _____

Author: _____

Reading Assignment: page _____ to page_____

Assignment:

Your job concerns the book's characters or content and the location. You will create some form of map representation of the reading content. The map can be a tracking map, a comparison map, or a collage or series of location maps. The question you are trying to answer is where is the content from the reading occurring? A **tracking map** is one that provides a visual display that follows or shows in order where events took place. A **comparison map** is one that shows your actual location relative to the material in the reading. The **map collage** would contain a collection of various maps of locations presented in the reading. In each case, you should edit the maps, such as adding marks onto the map image to specify location. Start by finding location information from the reading, noting where it occurs in the text and the locations that the text is describing. Now make your map. You can draw the map onto a sheet of paper from an atlas, then add marks, or waypoints, trackways, and character or event names onto the map to identify the reading location or locations. Once you have completed your map or maps, write a descriptive paragraph that explains your map materials.

What type of map are you creating?   ☐ Tracking   ☐ Comparison   ☐ Collage

Location notes

Page/Paragraph/Line	Location Statement
1	
2	
3	

Map Description: _____

_____

_____

_____

_____

Chapter 3

Electronic Text in the Literature Circle

The American Association of School Librarians (AASL) *Information Literacy Standards addressed in this chapter:*

- Information Literacy: 1 and 3
- Independent Learning: 5
- Social Responsibility: 7, 8, and 9

The International Society for Technology in Education (ISTE) Technology Foundation Standards for All Students addressed in this chapter:

- Basic operations and concepts: 1.1 and 1.2
- Social, ethical, and human issues: 2.3
- Technology productivity tools: 3.1
- Technology research tools: 5.1 and 5.3

For more information on these standards, see page ix.

In this chapter we will examine one facet of technology integration of the literature circle, that of using a technology-based book for the circle discussion. The electronic book, or eBook, can be used by a single student, a few students, a discussion group, or even a whole class depending on the needs of the students and the availability of the technology. *A listing of free eBook libraries is included at the end of this chapter.*

Electronic Forms of Text – the eBook

Electronic books, or eBooks, are among the newest forms of "reading materials" that we can use in our teaching tool kit. Reading is based on the technology of writing and printing, which has now evolved into an even higher technology format. When reviewing the history of reading, there is a recurrent trend of interest in the application of other technologies into reading (Kamil, Intrator, and Kim 2000). The recent development of computer and networking technologies have combined to provide new applications and interests in computer usage as applied to reading. Electronic books are textual documents that have been converted and "published" in an electronic format that display on eBook readers, devices or computers using eBook software programs. A modern definition is that an eBook is a digital text file, but not limited to just text, which is displayed on some form of computer or electronic device.

The electronic text can be used with standard literature circle activities. In this case, students' "Technology Activities" and the "Communications" between students could still be on the far left of the technology-enhanced continuum (see Figure 3.1). The use of digital versions of the reading material would move the student to the right side of the "Text Medium" category, although there is no reason why electronic books could not be used with technology-enhanced activities (Chapter 4), or with digital collaboration tools (Chapters 5 and 6).

Figure 3.1 Dimensions of using text display technology in the literature circle.

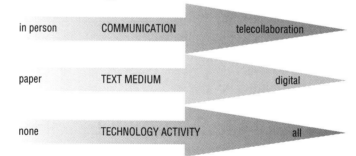

Technology-Enhanced Literature Circle

in person	COMMUNICATION	telecollaboration
paper	TEXT MEDIUM	digital
none	TECHNOLOGY ACTIVITY	all

Using electronic books and digital libraries can be excellent applications of existing technology. These tools allow students to read an eBook for enjoyment or research, or to use an eBook as a scaffold to improve their reading ability. Students can read eBooks from a hand-held computing device, a laptop, a desktop, many cell phones, or even an MP3 player. Using digital forms of text, parents, teachers, and schools can easily start integrating this form of books into a student's reading mediums. The paradigm of what a book is, and how we can use it, is shifting to include today's wide variety of paper-based print and technology-based digital book formats.

Studies have found that availability of books may be a key factor in reading achievement. Countries scoring higher in reading have students with greater access to books (Elley 1992). Krashen (1995) found a positive correlation between reading comprehension scores and number of books per student in library media centers. Using computers with reading instruction has also been found to assist in facilitating reading comprehension and increasing students' attitudes toward computer interactions (Kamil 2003). A number of students, including those with reading disabilities, can benefit from integrating technology into reading instruction using strategies such as text-to-speech, multimedia enhancements, and other interaction tools. Integrating electronic forms of books into the classroom will provide teachers and students an availability that has not existed before—24-hour, worldwide access to library media centers which present books in electronic form.

Advantages of eBooks

An existing problem for all schools and teachers has been that books are becoming increasingly expensive, quickly outdated, and physically cumbersome. To move from paper-based books to integrated digital media offers advantages of cost savings, efficiency, better accessibility, and enhancing or scaffolding reading tools and formats that engage the millennial student (U.S. DOE 2004). In many situations, the cost of books has risen in the double digits. For example, between 1983 and 1993, college textbook costs increased over 90%, and since 1998 textbook costs have risen an additional 41% (Schumer 2003; Toner 1998; Montclair State 2000; Christendom College 2003). Current estimates have the number of free books available on the Internet at over 100,000. While many eBooks do cost, the large number of free books makes using eBooks with students in class a cost-effective option for many educators who are trying to expand a classroom or school collection. An additional benefit is that books that have passed into the public domain are available as eBooks and can be given away to teachers, students, families, and anyone else at no cost.

A quote in the U.S. DOE's report *Toward a New Golden Age in American Education* (2004) exemplifies one of the frustrations of today's students, "I think that students should have laptops to do everything in class…we should not have to carry heavy books all day long and bring all of our books home" (20-21). A research project done concerning the weight of a middle school student's book bag found that the average weight of the bag was about twenty pounds—too much for a small child (Petracco 2001). Using computers and Internet access can allow any student to have access to thousands of books from online libraries and other book collections with no additional weight and without taking up any more shelf space in the classroom or library media center.

Some Common eBook Formats

While there are over 25 different formats of eBooks, this book will focus on five that are available without cost: text (.txt); Web (htm/.html/.xml); Adobe Acrobat Reader (.pdf); Microsoft Reader (.lit); and Palm eReader (.pdb). These formats use free programs that can access thousands of free eBooks appropriate for student use.

Software and files for eBooks come in a variety of formats. Some eBook programs are platform or device specific while many others are cross platform and can be viewed on a number of devices (see Table 3.1). HTML or text-based eBooks are ready to use in any standard Internet browser (see Figure 3.2). Using the browser program options, readers can adjust text style, size, and color. With HTML or text eBooks, it is possible to search for words or terms within the book file, and copy and paste selected text to other programs. The Adobe Reader PDF program has page navigation, multiple viewing options, searching, and the ability to add bookmarks and notes (see Figure 3.3). Many consider the Adobe Portable Document Format (PDF) a standard for electronic distribution worldwide, as pdf files are compact and can be easily shared, viewed, navigated, and printed. Palm eBooks can be read on Palm handheld devices and standard computers (see Figure 3.4). The Palm format has controls for backgrounds, fonts and font sizes, which controls the amount of text on the screen. Microsoft Reader eBooks are compatible with Windows operating systems for desktop and laptop computers as well as handheld devices (see Figure 3.5). The MS Reader program also has navigation controls, a portrait display format, controls for text size, and the ability to interact with the text by bookmarking, highlighting, note taking, and even drawing.

Table 3.1 Formats and associated devices for eBooks.

	Text	Web (html/xml)	Adobe Acrobat Reader	Microsoft Reader	Palm eReader
Windows desktops	Yes	Yes	Yes	Yes	Yes
Windows laptops	Yes	Yes	Yes	Yes	Yes
Apple desktops	Yes	Yes	Yes	No	Yes
Apple laptops	Yes	Yes	Yes	No	Yes
Windows handheld	Yes	Yes	Yes	Yes	Yes
Palm handhelds	Yes	Yes	Yes	No	Yes

Figure 3.2 *Jane Eyre* eBook, using a Web browser (Internet Explorer).

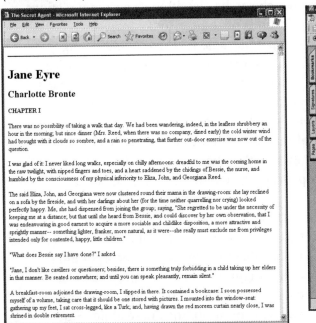

Figure 3.3 *Of Human Bondage* eBook, using Adobe Reader software.

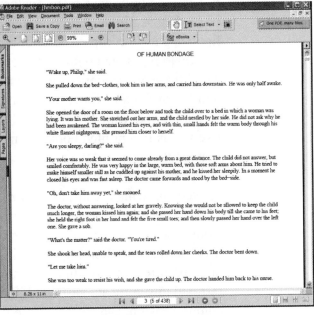

Figure 3.4 *20,000 Leagues Under the Sea* eBook, using Palm eReader software.

Figure 3.5 *Great Expectations* eBook, using MS Reader software.

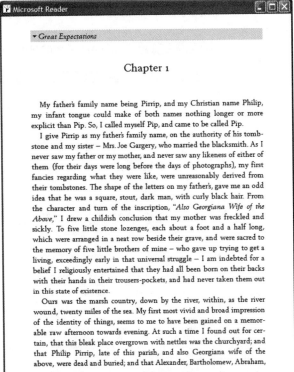

Technology-Based Reading Scaffolds

Electronic books have many features which can be classified as accommodations or reading scaffolds. Accommodating features of some eBooks include: lightweight (in comparison to other texts), adjustable text size, highlighting, bookmarking, note taking, interactive dictionaries, and read-aloud capabilities. The Microsoft Reader eBook format is the one I have found to have the greatest number of features for ease of use and for accommodations. MS Reader uses a display format called "ClearType" which makes text displayed on a screen look like words in a printed book. Some of the other features of MS Reader include a graphic that displays the reader's location within the book, a navigation system that remembers where the reader stops reading, and the last place that was viewed, allowing for instant return.

The text of most eBook programs is adaptable, allowing users to select from a variety of sizes and font styles to set the most comfortable display for the user (see Figures 3.6a-b). According to Elizabeth Lowe (2003), incorporating large print text into reading programs for struggling and reluctant readers has resulted in significant sustained improvement in word recognition/accuracy, comprehension, and fluency—the three forms of disabilities in reading. Students who struggle with reading, regardless of the reason, have been found to benefit from changing to larger font sizes, such as 14 or 16 point, as a reading scaffold. Use of large print does not have to be limited to those with visual difficulties. Larger font sizes and spacing can help students by causing their eyes to move more slowly while they read, thereby allowing students to track their reading more easily (Bloodsworth 1993) and giving them more processing time.

Figure 3.6a-b Small text and large text displayed with an eBook.

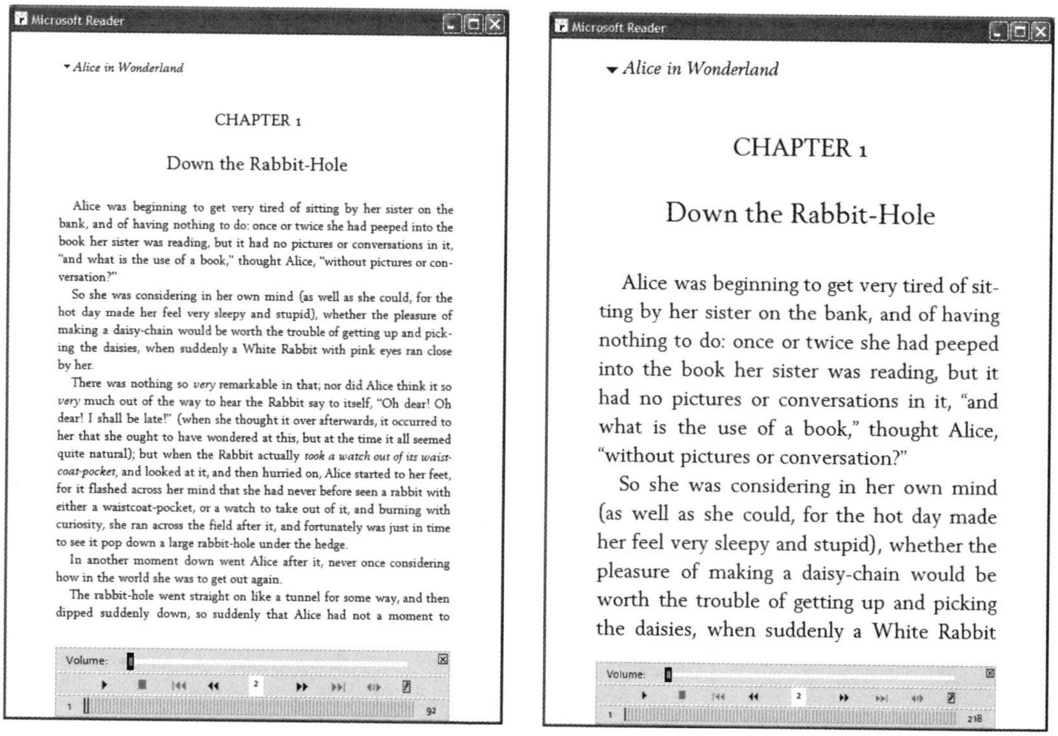

Figure 3.7 Highlighting ability in MS Reader.

Microsoft Reader

▾ *Alice in Wonderland*

with pink eyes ran close by her.

There was nothing so *very* remarkable in that; nor did Alice think it so *very* much out of the way to hear the Rabbit say to itself, "Oh dear! Oh dear! I shall be late!" (when she thought it over afterwards, it occurred to her that she ought to have wondered at this, but at the time it all seemed quite natural); but when the Rabbit actually *took a watch out of its waistcoat-pocket*, and looked at it, and then hurried on, Alice started to her feet, for it flashed across her mind that she had never before seen a rabbit with either a waist-coat-pocket, or a watch to take out of it, and burning with curiosity, she ran across the field after it, and fortunately was just in time to see it pop down a large rabbit-hole under the hedge.

Volume:

Figure 3.8 Internal drawing ability using MS Reader.

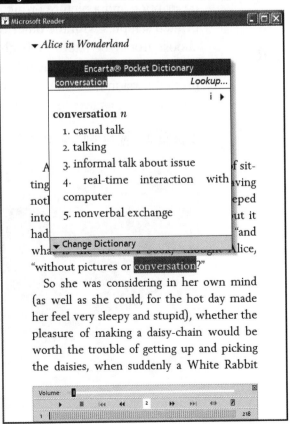

Microsoft Reader

▾ *Alice's Adventures in Wonderland*

A Caucus-Race and a Long Tale

THEY were indeed a queer-looking party that assembled on the bank--the birds with draggled feathers, the animals with their fur clinging close to them, and all dripping wet, cross, and uncomfortable.

The first question of course was, how to get dry again: they had a consultation about this, and after a few minutes it seemed quite natural to Alice to find herself talking familiarly with them, as if she had known them all her life, she had quite a long argument with the Lory, who at last turned sulky, and would only say, "I am older than you, and must know better"; and this Alice would not allow without knowing how old it was, and, as the Lory positively refused to tell its age, there was no more to be said.

At last the Mouse, who seemed to be a person of authority among them, called out, "Sit down, all of you, and listen to me! I'll soon make you dry enough!" They all sat down at once, in a large ring, with the Mouse in the middle. Alice kept her eyes anxiously fixed on it, for she felt sure she would catch a bad cold if she did not get dry very soon.

"Ahem!" said the Mouse with an important air. "Are you all ready? This is the driest thing I know. Silence all round, if you please! William the Conqueror, whose cause was favoured by the pope, was soon submitted to by the English, who wanted leaders, and had been of late much accustomed to usurpation and conquest. Edwin and Morcar, the earls of Mercia and Northumbria--"

"Ugh!" said the Lory, with a shiver.

"I beg your pardon!" said the Mouse, frowning, but very politely. "Did you speak?"

"Not I!" said the Lory hastily.

"I thought you did," said the Mouse.--"I proceed. 'Edwin and Morcar, the earls of Mercia and Northumbria, declared for him: and even

◂ 16 ▸

Done ■ Undo

Figure 3.9 Note taking ability in MS Reader.

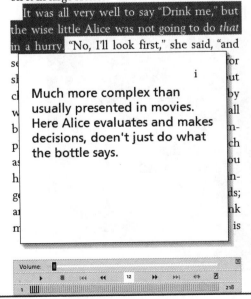

Microsoft Reader

▾ *Alice in Wonderland*

was not here before," said Alice,) and round the neck of the bottle was a paper label, with the words "DRINK ME" beautifully printed on it in large letters.

It was all very well to say "Drink me," but the wise little Alice was not going to do *that* in a hurry. "No, I'll look first," she said, "and

i

Much more complex than usually presented in movies. Here Alice evaluates and makes decisions, doesn't just do what the bottle says.

Volume:

Figure 3.10 MS Reader's interactive dictionary.

Microsoft Reader

▾ *Alice in Wonderland*

Encarta® Pocket Dictionary

conversation   Lookup...

i ▸

conversation *n*

1. casual talk
2. talking
3. informal talk about issue
4. real-time interaction with computer
5. nonverbal exchange

▾ Change Dictionary

"without pictures or conversation?"

So she was considering in her own mind (as well as she could, for the hot day made her feel very sleepy and stupid), whether the pleasure of making a daisy-chain would be worth the trouble of getting up and picking the daisies, when suddenly a White Rabbit

Volume:

The MS Reader eBook program also creates an annotation file that tracks where the reader is and stores reader-created bookmarks, highlights, drawings, and notes (see Figure 3.7-9). Microsoft also gives away free interactive dictionaries which, when placed in the eBook library, allow students to instantly look up words just by clicking on them with a mouse (see Figure 3.10). Along with these interactive features, the page display of the eBook itself is well designed, including margins to increase reading comfort, and a portrait page layout that displays a whole page at a time (no scrolling), with the option to black out the rest of the computer screen.

Reading aloud to children helps build listening, vocabulary, memory, and language skills and helps children learn information about the world around them (The Family Literacy Foundation 2002). Technology can assist teachers and students in integrating multiple modalities and learning styles through reading aloud. Many eBook programs integrate text-to-speech programs so that students can have a book read aloud by the computer. Text-to-speech programs of today do not just read word by word in a monotone, but look at the sentence for context, such as past, present, or future tense of words, and vary the tonality of the speech.

Using eBooks in the Literature Circle

You can incorporate eBooks into a standard classroom literature circle without much work; it is mostly a matter of integrating eBooks with the existing books available to students.

One method is to have "printed" sections of eBooks available with other printed books. This can be a chapter from a book or a contact sheet with a description and a picture or pictures from pages of a picture book. Place these printed samples with the other books that students can browse through and choose from (see later in this chapter for how to create printed chapters and contact sheets). Some students may prefer to read an electronic version over a printed version or desire or need the additional reading supports available with eBooks, such as text-to-speech audio support. If a class book is also available as

Figure 3.11 Stickers on printed books indicating eBook option.

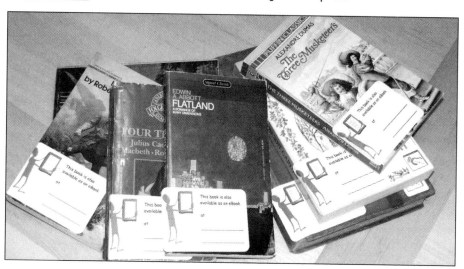

an eBook or audio book, stickers placed on the outside or inside cover of the class books can let students know of the digital option and provide them with the Web address or location of the eBook. Stickers can be made from mailing labels or other label sets and can be purchased from most office supply and department stores (see Figure 3.11 for sample stickers).

Selecting eBooks for Class

You can start finding electronic books for your classes by looking through the online electronic libraries. Many of the books will be copyright free, meaning they are old enough (pre-1920s) to have passed into the public domain. Anyone can freely copy, print, and distribute these books' contents. Using these books can be a cost-effective strategy for stretching a book budget (if you have one). In one situation, by searching through these electronic libraries, over 80 free eBooks that were on one state's reading list were found (Cavanaugh 2003).

While you will need to judge the eBooks yourself for class appropriateness and level, there are tools that can assist in this evaluation. A number of free readability analysis tools are available. If you are using MS Word for word processing, you can run a readability analysis with a spell check, or use online tools such as Using English.com (<http://www.usingenglish.com/resources/text-statistics.php>), OKAPI! (<http://www.interventioncentral.org/htmdocs/tools/okapi/okapi.shtml>), and Textalyser (<http://textalyser.net>).

To run a Flesch-Kincaid grade level and reading ease readability analysis with MS Word:

Figure 3.12 Readability analysis run on portion of text from *Alice in Wonderland.*

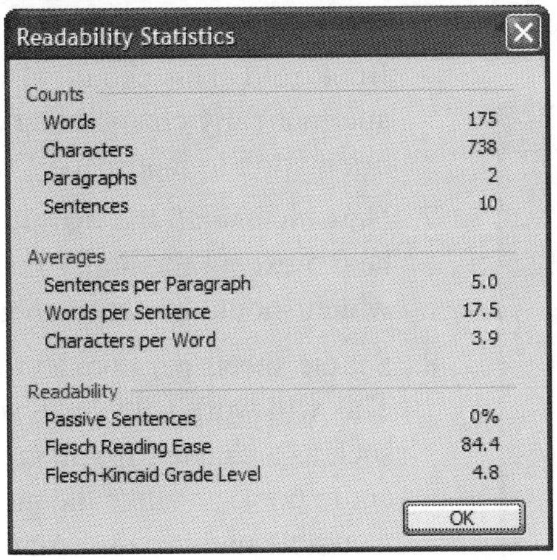

Readability Statistics	
Counts	
Words	175
Characters	738
Paragraphs	2
Sentences	10
Averages	
Sentences per Paragraph	5.0
Words per Sentence	17.5
Characters per Word	3.9
Readability	
Passive Sentences	0%
Flesch Reading Ease	84.4
Flesch-Kincaid Grade Level	4.8

1. Copy text from the eBook into a Word document.

2. From the **Tools** menu, select **Options**. Now switch to the **Spelling and Grammar** tab. Check the last box on the tab that says run **Readability** and click OK.

3. Run a **Spelling and Grammar** check and the readability analysis will appear when the spell check is finished (see Figure 3.12).

How to Print a Sample Book Chapter

Public domain books can be printed in total, if desired. Many other books also allow sections to be printed: check with a library media specialist about fair use limits for allowable amounts. To have printed samples of books for students to review, I would suggest that you do it a chapter or so at a time. Printing out just a chapter or two can get a student started or interested in a text. It is possible to use word processing programs such as MS Word to create booklets that have four book pages on a single sheet of paper (see Figure 3.13). Word will also arrange the pages and assist you in printing on both sides.

To make a booklet of a chapter using MS Word:

Figure 3.13 First chapters (samples) created from online books.

Figure 3.14 Page setup pop-up in MS Word.

1. Download or open an eBook in a text or html format.

2. Highlight and copy one or two chapters.

3. Start MS Word and create a new blank document.

4. Paste in the chapters by selecting **Paste** from the **Edit** menu.

5. You will now need to adjust the settings so that the booklet can be printed. Start by selecting **Page Setup** from the **File** menu (see Figure 3.14).

6. In the **Page Setup** pop-up under the margins tab, start by changing the **Multiple pages** setting dropdown to **Book fold**. This should also automatically change the page orientation to landscape.

7. Now change all the margin values to be 0.5 except the gutter margin which should be set to about 0.25.

8. Set the sheets per booklet to be *all.* This will work with small sections, such as a chapter. If you are printing entire books, change the number to a workable number for assembling, such as 20, or it will get to be too thick to fold effectively.

9. Once the settings are complete, click the **OK** button.

10. You might want to add page numbers to your booklet. Do this by selecting **Insert Page Numbers** from the **Insert** menu.

11. If you want to have the book title at the top of every page, you can add it to the header. Select **Header and Footer** from the **View** menu and then type in the desired information.

12. Now select **Print** from the **File** menu.

13. In the **Print** pop-up you will need to make a few choices. First make sure that the **Collate box** is checked. If your printer can print automatically on both sides, you are ready to print; if not you will need to place a check in the **Manual duplex** box. With manual duplex, a page will print, and then you will need to place the same page back in your printer so the second side can be printed. You might need to practice some to be sure that the page is in the right orientation and side up.

14. Click the **OK** button to start printing.

15. You can create a cover for your booklet by creating a new document. With the page in the landscape format, create two text boxes on each side of the page. In the right box write in the title, author, eBook URL or location, and any other information and then insert a good (relative) picture. In the left text box, write a short description of the book's topic. Print this page on card stock to make a good book cover.

16. Once all the printing is done, covers and inside, place the pages together and fold in the middle to make your booklet. You may wish to bind the booklet with staples or some other material.

Figure 3.15 Sample booklet in word processor before printing of a single chapter of *The Secret Garden.*

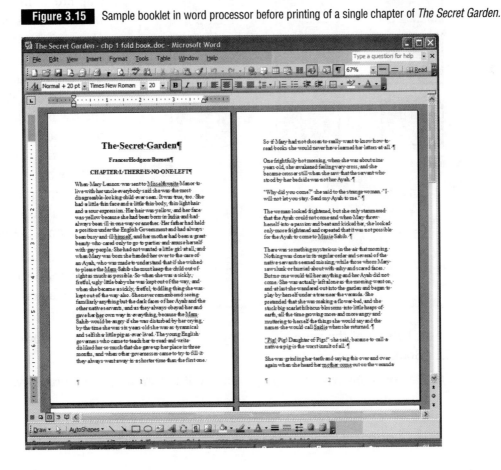

How to Print a Contact Sheet for a Picture Book

Some sites such as the Children's International Digital Library already have display pages that are contact sheets (see Figure 3.16). These sheets display all of the pages of a book as thumbnail images. A teacher could print one of these Web pages and place it with the other picture books. It would be better to print the page on a sheet of card stock and laminate it for durability.

Another way to create a sheet for a picture book is to use a word processor:

Figure 3.16 Book overview Web page from *The Children's Object Book,* courtesy of the International Children's Digital Library Web site at the University of Maryland, with permission from the U.S. Library of Congress.

1. Start with a new blank page.

2. Write the title and author of the book in large print at the top of the page.

3. Write a brief description of the book, such as you might find on the back cover, describing the story and characters.

4. Capture an image from the book and place this at the bottom of the sheet. You can capture an image from a Web site by using the print screen button on the keyboard, switch back to the word processing program, and then paste the image onto the page.

5. Use the drawing or image tools to crop out unwanted sections of the image.

6. At the bottom of the page either copy or paste in the Web address or describe the eBook location.

7. Print the page on card stock and laminate it for strength and durability.

Electronic Book (eBook) Circle

Another strategy for using eBooks for discussion circles is to have an eBook group, where all members of the group read the same eBook. You will need to have a sufficient number of computers or reading devices for the group to use. There will also need to be a variety of eBooks for students to choose from covering various topics and at different reading levels. Have students make their selection from a list of books, including eBooks, and then sort their selections. Now create a group of students that chose books that exist as eBooks. The educator can work with that group to provide instruction on how to use the eBooks while the group performs the same activities as the other groups who are reading paper-based text.

Electronic books can also be used to expand the classroom experience to include a student's home and possibly family. Posting a list of links to appropriate eBooks on a class site can make more books available to the student and can be used to encourage parent/student reading. This can also be a way for a teacher to provide students access to books without needing as many printed copies of the text.

Teacher Applications

Classroom teachers may also wish to use eBooks, for example, as big books and for reading assessment probes, tying the material from the literature circle reading back into the class instruction. Using an eBook and a video projector a teacher can instantly create a digital "Big Book" on a screen for use with a class. He can use the eBook to illustrate passages or demonstrate how reading samples may be used in the literature circle. The teacher can also use eBook contents to create reading assessments, such as Curriculum Based Assessment (CBA) Reading Probes based upon literature circle reading. To create a CBA Reading Probe from an eBook, the educator will need to have Web access, an eBook, and a printer.

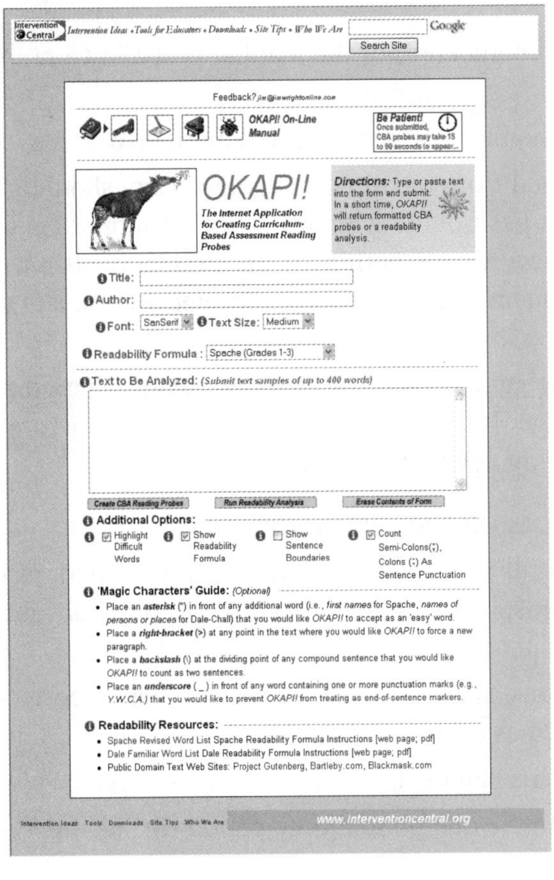

To create the reading probe based on a literature circle reading:

1. Select a passage from an eBook that is about 100 to 200 words (the maximum is 200 words). A quick way to do this is to

Figure 3.17 OKAPI! Web site for creating CBA Reading Probes.

copy and paste passages into a word processing program, such as MS Word, and use the **Word Count** option from the **Tools** menu.

2. Once you have found a few passages you would like to use, go to the OKAPI! Web site at <http://www.interventioncentral.org/htmdocs/tools/ okapi/okapi.shtml> (see Figure 3.17).

3. Copy and paste the eBook passage into the appropriate spot on the OKAPI! site.

4. Select the option to run a readability analysis on the passage: you can select either Spache for elementary grades one through three or Dale-Chall for grades four and above. This analysis will print out on the teacher/examiner page.

5. Now have the site create the examiner and student pages by clicking on the Create CBA Reading Probes button, and then print out the pages.

6. Laminate or place the student and teacher sheets in clear sheet pockets for protection and storage. By laminating the sheets a teacher can use a whiteboard marker or overhead pen to mark on his sheet as the student reads, and then erase and reuse with another student.

How to use the reading probe:

This form of reading probe is an evaluation tool designed to establish ability. To complete the probe, the student will read their page for one minute. The reading probe identifies in a student reading abilities of word identification, recognition capacity, and comprehension skills. The instructor totals and evaluates the number of words read and understood by the student.

Using the reading probe:

1. Place the student copy (unnumbered) of the reading probe in front of the student.

2. Use the teacher copy to monitor performance and mark errors.

3. Have the student read aloud from the top of the page. They should try to read every word. If the student has trouble with any word for more than three seconds, supply them the word. Say nothing if the student reads a word incorrectly—note that student self-corrections, repeated words, and dialect characteristics are not errors.

4. After one minute have the student stop and mark the word where the student stops on the instructor page. If the student finished their page before the time is up, have him start reading again from the beginning.

Record student actions and errors on the instructor page:

1. Put a slash (/) through words read incorrectly (errors). Also mark as incorrect: teacher-supplied words, mispronunciations, word omissions, substitutions, and words read out of sequence.

2. Circle unusual proper nouns, such as names, which are read incorrectly— these are not to be counted as errors.

3. Mark word insertions with a caret (^).

4. Mark the last word read in the one minute time period by placing a bracket after the word (]).

Scoring the reading probe:

Words per minute: Use the word count numbers from each line to add to the number of words on the next line up to the bracket to find the score.

Total Words Correct (TWC): Subtract the number of reading error words (/) from the total words read.

Reading Errors: Add the number of reading error words (/) and the number of word insertions (^).

Electronic books can be an effective resource for any classroom or library media center. Electronic texts come in a variety of formats, each with a variety of abilities that can assist with student learning. This chapter helped identify for educators some of the features and uses that can make eBooks effective tools in the general educational experience and specifically with literature circles. Additionally, while educators can use electronic texts in a classroom with print material, some strategies, scaffolds, and applications can be better applied to realize the potential of electronic versions of print resources with students. Take some time to explore eBooks and the possibilities for use within a classroom and school.

References

Bloodsworth, J. G. (1993). Legibility of print (Report No. CS-011-244). East Lansing, MI: National Center for Research on Teacher Learning. (ERIC Document Reproduction Service No. ED355497). Electronic version retrieved October 2004 from <http://www.eric.ed.gov>.

Cavanaugh, Terence. "EBooks – an Unknown Reading Option," paper presented at Society for Information Technology and Teacher Education (SITE) Conference, Albuquerque, NM (2003).

Cristendom College. "Fees and Financial Aid." Christendom College (2003). Retrieved October 2003 from <http://www.christendom.edu/admissions/feesfaid.shtml#books>.

Elley, W. B. (1992) How in the World Do Students Read? The IEA Study of Reading Literacy. The Hague, the Netherlands: International Association for the Evaluation of Educational Achievement.

Family Literacy Foundation (2002) . Why Read Aloud with Children? Retrieved October 2004 from <http://www.read2kids.org/documents/whyreadaloud.pdf>.

Kamil, M. L., S. Intrator, and H. S. Kim. "Effects of other technologies on literacy and literacy learning." In M. Kamil, P. Mosenthal, P. D. Person, et al. (Eds.) *Handbook of Reading Research* Vol. 3: 773-788. Mahwah, NF: Lawerence Erlbaum Associates (2000).

Kamil, Michael L. "Adolescents and Literacy: Reading for the 21st Century." *Alliance for Excellent Education* (2003). Retrieved April 2005 from <http://www.all4ed.org/publications/AdolescentsAndLiteracy.pdf>.

Krashen, S. (1995). School Libraries, Public Libraries, and the NAEP Reading Scores. School Library Media Quarterly, 23.

Lowe, E. (2003). Large Print Books: The Missing Link for Speed and Fluency for All Students—Struggling, Proficient, in Between. Paper presented at the International Reading Association Conference, Orlando, FL.

Montclair State University. "Faculty urged to meet textbook adoption deadline." *INSIGHT* (2000). Retrieved October 2003 from <http://www.montclair.edu/pages/Publications/Insight/BackIssues/2000/Insight041000/story2.html>.

Petracco, Patricia A. "Weighing in on Backpacks." School Leader Info Link, *School Leader* (2001). Retrieved January 2004 from <http://www.njsba.org/members_only/publications/school_leader/May-June-2001/info_link.htm>.

Schumer, Charles E. "Senator Schumer Reveals Local College Textbook Prices Are Skyrocketing – And Proposes New $1,000 Tax Deduction To Help Cover Cost." Press Release (2003). Retrieved October 2003 from <http://www.senate.gov/~schumer/SchumerWebsite/pressroom/press_releases/PR02067.html>.

Toner, Erin. "Tax Break, State Priorities Debated." *The State News* (1998). Retrieved October 2003 from <http://www.statenews.com/editionsspring98/020398/p1_commit.html>.

U.S. Department of Education (USDOE), Office of Educational Technology (OET). Toward a New Golden Age in American Education: How the Internet, the Law and Today's Students Are Revolutionizing Expectations [Electronic Version]. Washington, D. C., 2004. Retrieved April 2005 from <http://www.ed.gov/about/offices/list/os/technology/plan/2004/plan.pdf>.

Web Resources: eBooks and eBook Libraries

The following is a list of sites of free online eBook libraries and other resources which can be used to obtain eBooks for classes. This list is by no means exhaustive and searches can be done to find more books. Visit **www.drscavanaugh.org/ebooks/** for an updated list of free eBook libraries.

Children's Online Libraries

Aesop's Fables
<http://www.umass.edu/aesop/contents.html>
Thirty-eight fables in traditional and modern forms. Most in HTML, some in FLASH.

Amazing Adventure Series
<http://www.amazingadventure.com/>
Children's stories which can be read on the screen or read aloud, with two books in FLASH format.

arts-entertainment-recreation.com
<http://www.arts-entertainment-recreation-com/Arts/Literature/Children's_Literature/Online_Books/>
Links to a variety of online children's books.

BAB Books
<http://www.sundhagen.com/babbooks/>
Over 12 online html picture books.

BookPals – performing artists for literacy in schools
   <http://www.bookpals.net/storyline/>
   Eleven stories read by members of the screen actors guild (and others). Stories are read and displayed in a video screen (Windows Media, Real, & Quicktime). Additional story is available by phone (<http://www.bookpals.net/storyline/phone.html>).

Book-Pop
   <http://www.bookpop.com/bookpop.html>
   Twelve HTML picture books with the option to have the book read aloud.

byGosh.com
   <http://www.bygosh.com/index.html>
   Children's classic books in HTML format.

Candlelight Stories
   <http://www.candlelightstories.com/stories.asp>
   Children's and chapter books in a variety of formats.

CBeebies Story Circle
   <http://www.bbc.co.uk/cbeebies/storycircle/>
   Over 80 FLASH and printable books.

Children's Books Online
   The Rosetta Project, Inc. (formerly Editec Communications' Children's Books for Free library) <www.childrensbooksonline.org>
   One thousand, two hundred antique children's books published in the nine-teenth and early twentieth centuries, in HTML.

Children's StoryBooks Online
   <http://www.magickeys.com/books/>
   Over 20 illustrated childrens stories in HTML.

Class Conscious Big Books
   <http://www.classconsciousbooks.com/big%20books.htm>
   Seventeen young children's stories, HTML based.

Clifford's Interactive Storybooks
   <http://teacher.scholastic.com/clifford1/>
   Four interactive stories about Clifford the Big Red Dog in FLASH format, presented by Scholastic.

International Children's Digital Library (ICDL)
   <http://www.icdlbooks.org/>
   The ICDL is building an international collection that reflects both the diversity and quality of children's literature from 27 cultures in 23 languages (HTML).

Internet Public Library – KidSpace
   <http://www.ipl.org/div/kidspace/>
   This section of IPL contains The Reading Zone, which is similar to the fiction section at a public library. There are links to online stories and information and links about favorite books and authors.

Kiz Club
   <http://www.kizclub.com/Sbody.html>
   Forty-four leveled FLASH books with printable versions.

Mighty Book Catalogue

<http://www.mightybook.com/catalogue.htm>
Over 50 children's books ages two to preteen, in HTML. Books will read aloud.

NASA Books Imagers

<http://imagers.gsfc.nasa.gov/>
Online stories *Echo the Bat* and *Amelia the Pigeon* in HTML.
Robin Whirlybird on her Rotorcraft Adventures <http://rotored.arc.nasa.gov>
A story and activities of a girl visiting her mother's work. Available in English, Spanish, and Chinese (HTML).
Our Very Own Star and Auroras! (FLASH format)
<http://stargazer.gsfc.nasa.gov/epo/jsp/products.jsp>

RIF Reading Planet

<http://www.rif.org/readingplanet/content/read_aloud_stories.mspx>
A collection of read aloud books that changes monthly (FLASH format).

Sebastian Swan's Infant Explorer

<http://www.naturegrid.org.uk/infant/>
Eight online big books (HTML).

Sesame Street

<http://www.sesameworkshop.org/sesamestreet/sitemap/?sectionId=stories> Read and make stories (FLASH).

Stories to Read Online

<http://www.beenleigss.qld.edu.au/requested_sites/storiesontheWeb/
storiesontheWeb.html>
A collection links to young children's stories.

StoryPlace Elementary Library

<http://www.storyplace.org/eel/other.asp>
Six FLASH-formatted stories with associated activities and suggested readings.

StoryPlace PreSchool Library

<http://www.storyplace.org/preschool/other.asp>
Fifteen FLASH-formatted stories with associated activities for children and parents.

Tales of Wonder

<http://www.darsie.net/talesofwonder/index.html>
Folk and fairy tales from around the world, in HTML.

United States of Americas Korean War Commemoration

<http://korea50.army.mil/teachers/index.shtml>
Two online picture books (HTML).

General Online Libraries

Abacci Books

<http://www.abacci.com/books/default.asp>
Digital text versions of classic literature with reviews from Amazon (txt & .lit).

Alex Catalog of Electronic Texts

<http://sunsite.berkeley.edu/alex> or <http://www.infomotions.com/alex/>
Site contains a catalog with roughly 2,000 links of e-texts, located on various servers.

Aportis Library
    <http://www.aportis.com/library/index.html>
    Over 5,000 "AportisDoc" or "DOC" format books.

Audio Books for Free
    <http://www.audiobooksforfree.com/screen_main.asp>
    Over 3,000 audio books (as MP3 files) available for free download. Some
    texts are available as unabridged editions.

Baen Free Library
    <http://www.baen.com/library/>
    Over 80 relatively new science fiction books in HTML, Reader, Palm,
    Rocket, and RTF.

Bartleby.com
    <http://www.bartleby.com/>
    Classic books and resource/reference texts in HTML.

Bibliomania
    <http://www.bibliomania.com/>
    Over 2,000 texts of classic literature, book notes, references, and resources in
    HTML format.

Blackmask Online
    <http://www.blackmask.com/>
    Over 10,000 texts in a variety of formats: .lit, .html, .pds, etc.

BookRags
    <http://www.bookrags.com/index.html>
    Book notes and over 1,500 novels (HTML) available.

Books2GoLibrary.com
    <http://www.books2golibrary.com/ebooks_free.html>
    Palm, Pocket PC or desktop PC eBooks.

CIA Publication Library
    <http://www.cia.gov/cia/publications/index.html>
    Includes the World Fact Book with information on every country in the world
    (HTML).

Classic Book Library
    <http://classicbook.info/index.html>
    Over 125 books in seven genres done in HTML page-by-page format.

CyberRead Free Books
    <http://www.cyberread.com/free_ebooks/free_catalg.asp>

Digital Text Project
    <http://www.ilt.columbia.edu/publication/digitext.html>
    Links to great books.

DotLit
    <http://www.dotlit.com/>
    MS Reader .lit files.

Electronic Text Center at the University of Virginia Library
    <http://etext.lib.virginia.edu/>
    Thousands of xml, html, Reader, and Palm texts.

Elegant Solutions Software Company eBooks
<http://esspc-ebooks.com/default.htm>
MS Reader books.

The English Server's Fiction Collection
<http://eserver.org/fiction/>
Works of and about fiction.

The Florida Electronic Library
<http://www.flelibrary.org/>
A full digital public library for Florida Residents.

The Franklin Free Library
<http://www.franklin.com/freelibrary/
One thousand-plus text and HTML files.

Free-Books.org
<http://www.free-books.org/>
Lots of books in both text and MP3 formats.

Free Library of Classics
<http://www.information-resources.com/Library/library.html>
  Over 200 HTML-formatted classics.

Internet Public Library
<http://www.ipl.org/div/books>
Links to over 20,000 titles.

LiteralSystems.org
<http://literalsystems.org/files/>
Over 45 audio eBooks of classic literature and poetry.

Litrix Reading Room
<http://www.litrix.com/readroom.htm>
Over 300 public domain titles in HTML chapter format.

Making of America (MOA)
<http://cdl.library.cornell.edu/moa/>
Created by Cornell University Library, MOA is a digital library of primary
sources in American social history (antebellum through reconstruction periods).
This is a full text/image journal site of 22 magazines from the 1830s to 1900s.

Manybooks.net
<http://manybooks.net/>
More than 10,000 eBooks for Palm, PocketPC, Zaurus, Rocketbook, or PDA
in multiple formats.

Online Books
<http://onlinebooks.library.upenn.edu/>
Fifteen thousand-plus listings, usually .txt.

Page-by-Page Books
<http://www.pagebypagebooks.com/>
About 400 books to be read online (HTML).

PitBooks.com
<http://www.pitbook.com/home.htm>
About 100 books in English and French grouped into a variety of topics.

PocketRocketFX.com
<http://www.pocketrocketfx.com/html/ebooks.htm>
Classics library in Reader format.

Project Gutenberg
<http://promo.net/pg/>
Oldest, and one of the largest, online libraries; format usually .txt only.

Read Print
<http://www.readprint.com/>
Thousands of books for students, teachers, and classic enthusiasts in HTML format.

WebBooks.com
<http://www.Web-books.com/default.htm>
Over 1,000 classic texts, usually in Reader format.

Wired for Books
<http://www.wiredforbooks.org/>
Collections of audio books and interviews. Contains full versions of *A Christmas Carol, Alice in Wonderland,* and *Beatrix Potter Stories* along with short stories and excerpts from other books (Real Player).

World eBook Library
<http://netlibrary.net/WorldHome.html>
Over 27,000 free eBooks in HTML format.

Foreign Language Online Libraries

Libros Tauro (Argentina)
<http://www.librostauro.com.ar/>
Spanish: Several thousand eBooks.

Biblioteca Virtual do Estudante Brasileiro:
<http://www.bibvirt.futuro.usp.br/index.html?principal.html&2>
Portuguese: Several hundred eBooks.

Athena Texts Francais
<http://un2sg4.unige.ch/athena/>
French: 10,000 eBooks (French & Swiss Authors) Literature, philosophy, history, economics, science, and more.

Goettingen State & University Library, Germany
<http://gdz.sub.uni-goettingen.de/search-entry.shtml>
German: Approximately 4,500 eBook titles, primarily in German, French, and English, devoted mostly to Exploration and Travel Literature and Mathematics (the English-Language titles are indexed).

Online Books Page Links to Foreign Language Libraries
<http://onlinebooks.library.upenn.edu/archives.html#foreign>
Links to over seventy foreign language libraries with languages ranging from Afghan to Czech, French to Russian, Latin to Yiddish.

Other Electronic Print Forms

UComics.com
<http://www.ucomics.com/comics/>
Over 60 daily newspaper comic strips.

Comics.com
<http://www.unitedmedia.com/categories/index.html>
Over 88 newspaper comic strips archived for the last 30 days.

Newspapers on the Internet
<http://www.ims.uni-stuttgart.de/info/Newspapers.html>
Listing of newspapers from around the world that can be read online.

Artbomb.net
<http://www.artbomb.net/comics.jsp#>
Five graphic novels.

Slate
<http://www.slate.com/>
An online magazine that is also published as an eBook.

eBook Search Tools

SearcheBooks
<http://www.searchebooks.com/>
SearcheBooks searches multiple full text book sites.

eBookLocator
<http://www.ebooklocator.com/
Search database of thousands of books.

Online Books Search Books Page
<http://onlinebooks.library.upenn.edu/search.html>
Search from over 20,000 listings.

Digital Book Index
<http://www.digitalbookindex.com/search001a.htm>
Index for most major eBook sites, along with thousands of smaller specialized sites.

Readability Tools

Using English.com
<http://www.usingenglish.com/resources/text-statistics.php>

OKAPI!
<http://www.interventioncentral.org/htmdocs/tools/okapi/okapi.shtml>

Textalyser
<http://textalyser.net>

Chapter *4*

Enhancing the Literature Circle with Technology

The American Association of School Librarians (AASL)
Information Literacy Standards addressed in this chapter:

- Information Literacy: 1, 2, and 3
- Independent Learning: 5
- Social Responsibility: 7 and 9

The International Society for Technology in Education (ISTE) Technology
Foundation Standards for All Students addressed in this chapter:

- Basic operations and concepts: 1.1 and 1.2
- Social, ethical, and human issues: 2.2 and 2.3
- Technology productivity tools: 3.1
- Technology communication tools: 4.2
- Technology research tools: 5.1 and 5.3

For more information on these standards, see page xi.

This chapter presents strategies for integrating technology into literature circle activities. These activities include technology integration in the areas of research, multimedia, and organization. Integrating technology within a literature circle can be done by a single student within a group, a whole discussion group, or a whole class, depending on the availability of the technology. A list of online research tools is included in this chapter.

Integrating Technology

Through the use of technology, such as computers and the Internet, students are provided opportunities to develop literacy skills through their collaborative work and interactions with each other (Kamil 2003). Technology offers additional mediums for communication and collaboration with tools such as e-mail, chat rooms, discussion forums, and blogs, where readers interact and collaborate with each other through written formats. The use of online discussions and interactions can develop communication and literacy skills. The International Reading Association (IRA 2002) recommends that today's teachers should ensure student access to technology, integrating the Internet and other information and communication technologies into the literacy curriculum, especially in developing literacies that apply to new information uses. Literacy and communication need to be rethought in education to allow for creativity in different domains and levels, promoting a multimodal literacy (Kress 2003). While students are interacting in person and can use a printed-on-paper or digital version of a book, enhancing the student roles with technology-based activities doesn't change the strategies or dynamics of the cooperative group. Integrating technology into the literature circle does change, or enhance, some or all of the student activities, as the "Activity" dimension is shifted more to the right depending on how many students are participating with technology enhancements (see Figure 4.1).

Figure 4.1 Dimensions of using technology in the literature circle.

none   TECHNOLOGY ACTIVITY   all

Classroom Technology Configurations

Technology literacy activities have students applying computing devices, such as handhelds, desktops, or laptops, to access and use information and communication technologies. Today's common classroom technology configurations include the networked or standalone one-computer classroom; a classroom with two or more computers, usually clustered in some part of the room; and the full computer lab design or some adaptation on the design using portable laptops or handhelds allowing one-to-one computing (Cavanaugh 2005). I integrated technology literacy with my students in a variety of classroom configurations, from a one-computer classroom to a full computer lab (see

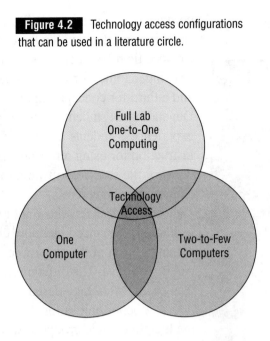

Figure 4.2). The resulting difference among these configurations was the amount of time each student could spend interacting with the technology.

Some common applications of technology in one-computer classrooms include the use of computers as a presentation tool by teachers or students, the use of a computer by the teacher to help manage his or her class, such as to help write letters and worksheets, track students with an electronic gradebook, and use it as a planning tool. But even a single computer in a classroom can be used by students as part of a literature circle activity. It can be a tool for individual input as part of a larger group project, as a learning center or research station, and even as a cooperative learning tool. Students can access a single computer to use an electronic atlas or encyclopedia, apply curriculum-supporting software, get reading and writing assistance, and even create as a class a database of characters from books, entered by students. To increase student access to the technology for their literature circle roles, consider sharing one or two of your computers with other teachers. Often a computer can be put on a cart and shared among teachers, a strategy that works very well with teaching teams. With greater access to technology, more options and access can be created in the classroom.

Technology Management

For technology-integrated strategies to flow smoothly, teachers should establish procedures for both managing the technology resources and student access to those technologies. Students can be allocated amounts of time on a rotation schedule to use the computer or computers for individual or group reading, research, or projects. Consider scheduling time on the computers for either individuals or groups. For example, a teacher can use a timer and a class roster next to the computer. Students set the timer for 10 to 15 minutes and then pass the timer to the next student on the list. Or a teacher can post a schedule and students from groups can rotate at 15-minute shifts. As a strategy for turn taking, teachers can hang a string horizontally with labels on each end of "been there" or "not yet" (see Figure 4.3). Then write either student or group names on clothespins and place them on the string. The labeled clothespins are placed appropriately to indicate if the student or group has had his or her turn at using that computer. Using one computer as a station, with pairs of students doing the same role from different groups, can be an effective cooperative learning activity.

To assist students who need help with the technology, experienced students can be used as student coaches. Teachers can also make information reference sheets or posters of common usage steps to place near the computer stations. With multiple

Figure 4.3 Clothesline strategy of tracking turns for computer usage.

computers, teachers can dedicate specific computers within the classroom for specific roles, such as one for drawing, another for Internet searching, and a third for concept mapping. Depending on students' abilities and experiences, students might need instruction for using removable media, network file storage, software, Internet sites, and audio controls.

For teachers who want to apply technology-enhanced literature circle activities, each of the classroom designs can be effective. The different classroom technology designs will offer different opportunities for students in the literature circle groups to work together, blending nontechnology roles with the technology roles. Student activities can range from having just one student from each group use the technology to having most of a class participate by using technology (see Table 4.1). Just because a classroom does not have full one-to-one computing options for all students doesn't mean a teacher can't incorporate technology-based activities into the literature circle design.

Table 4.1 Class designs and technology applications for technology-enhanced circles.

Class Design	Activities
One-computer class	Only a few roles (one or two) that use technology are assigned as part of the roles for each discussion group. Individuals from each group take turns using the technology.
Centers or two-to-few computers	Only a few roles (one or two) that use technology are assigned as part of the roles for each discussion group, and individuals from each group take turns using the technology. One of the class discussion groups is chosen to be the technology-based group, with that group doing mostly technology-based roles while the rest of the class has non-technology based roles.
Whole class or one-to-one computing	The whole class's discussion groups participate using technology-based roles. Groups are either assigned or given the option to be a technology-based role discussion group. Individual student technology-integrated roles are randomly spread through out the class.

Technology-Enhanced Literature Circle Roles

In terms of the literacy instruction and classroom design, blending technology with literature circles is a method or strategy that students can use to share their reading experiences, and at the same time, integrate technology. By integrating technology with the literature circle concept, students and teachers can expand beyond the classroom to access a worldwide audience for sharing and using resources and tools, which can assist students in obtaining, organizing, analyzing, and communicating (Lamb, Smith and Johnson 1999). Using a technology-enhanced literature circle allows readers to still experience standard literature circle concepts and strategies with value added by technology integrations that require students to use technology tools as they apply to today's literacies. Technology-based activity roles include digital technology applications of search and research, multimedia, and using technology for organization (see Table 4.2).

A set of technology-enhanced literature circle role sheets is provided at the end of this chapter.

Table 4.2 The technology-enhanced literature circle roles, their technology applications, and ISTE standards.

Technology Application Area	Role	Technology	Tech Foundation Standard (ISTE)
Search & Research	Vocabulary Elaborator	Interactive Dictionary	1,2,4,6
		Online dictionaries	1,2,4,6
	Background Researcher	Internet research	1, 2, 5
		Search engines	1, 2, 5
	Web Researcher	Ask an expert	1, 2, 5, 6
		Author study/Ask an author	1, 2, 5, 6
Multimedia	Literary Expository	Audio recording	1, 2, 4
	Graphic Illustrator	Paint	1, 2, 3, 4
	Media Hunter	Multimedia search engines	1, 2, 5
Organization	Graphic Organizer	Mind/concept mapping software	1, 2, 3, 4
		Concept map Web sites	1, 2, 3, 5
	Mapper/Tracker	Online research	1, 2, 3, 5
		Desktop publishing	1, 3, 4

These technology enhancements for literature circle roles use technology tools that are available or can be installed on a standard classroom computer with Internet access. These role activities were designed to use tools such as word processors, Internet browsers, and basic multimedia tools. Some of the specific role assignments related to searching and research involve students using a variety of Web applications, including accessing different kinds of search engines and going to specific Web sites, such as encyclopedia and atlas sites, to do research. Multimedia role assignments involve students using various multimedia software programs to create drawings using digital paint or drawing tools, to make audio recordings of themselves reading passages, and to create collages of images using desktop publishing. Organizing activities include students using either concept mapping software programs or Web sites, which can help students organize information. The technology use does not have to be limited to student roles. With technology-enhanced literature circles, teachers can use either print or digital forms of books with their students.

Educator Collaboration

The technology-enhanced literature circle provides an excellent opportunity for collaboration between teachers and library media specialists, as library media specialists teach both teachers and students new technology skills. Library media specialists can collaborate with a teacher, creating a cooperative partnership involving technology. Working with the classroom teacher, a library media specialist can provide instruction and assistance in the instruction and integration of literacy, and the National Education Technology Standards (NETS), to students as they do projects such as technology-enhanced literature circles. Today's students need knowledge concerning how to effectively research. Library media specialists are excellent resources who can provide instruction to students and teachers in using technology resources and locating information physically in the library media center, using databases, and online.

The library media specialist can be a strong support member of an educational team in creating an effective literature circle. She can work with teachers to find available texts in print and online for students to choose from when preparing reading material for literature circles. She can also assist by coordinating between a classroom teacher and a computer lab teacher or lab manager so that students can have whole class lab access for one-to-one computing opportunities with the technology. If whole class scheduling is not possible, the library media specialist can work with teachers to set up schedules so that single students or groups of students can use computers in the library media center or other computers in the school as part of their class.

The library media specialist can adapt the library media center to be more accommodating to student technology access. She can organize space within the physical library media center by creating centers for literature circle discussion or identifying computers for literature circle use. As library media specialists are often responsible for the school Web presence, they can also set up school Web pages with resources for online research, research instruction, and electronic book locations.

Classroom Scenarios

The following are three classroom examples showing how technology-enhanced roles can be integrated into literature circle activities. In each case, the technology is applied in different ways, from only a few students using the technology to whole class one-to-one computing.

Elementary School: Imaginary Worlds

Ms. Heia teaches an upper elementary class of 25 students in an urban school. She has chosen a theme of imaginary worlds for her next class literature circle activity. Working with the library media specialist to identify high-interest books available in sufficient numbers, Ms. Heia has selected the following books as choices for the reading activity:

- *A Wrinkle in Time* by Madeleine L'Engle
- *Artemis Fowl* by Eoin Colfer
- *Castle in the Attic* by Elizabeth Winthrop
- *Ella Enchanted* by Gail Carson Levine
- *Indian in the Cupboard* by Lynne Reid Banks
- *The Lion, the Witch, and the Wardrobe* by C. S. Lewis

To introduce the topic to students, she reads excerpts from some of the books and plays professionally read excerpts from the Random House Web site (<http://www.randomhouse.com/>) for *Ella Enchanted* and *Artemis Fowl*. Single copies of the books are left out for a day for students to peruse before making their ordered list of book discussion choices. Ms. Heia collects the student choices and uses those choices to create five or six reading groups of four or five students each. Ms. Heia plans to have the students read their books daily as part of their sustained silent reading time, and then have the discussion groups meet weekly.

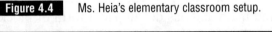

Figure 4.4   Ms. Heia's elementary classroom setup.

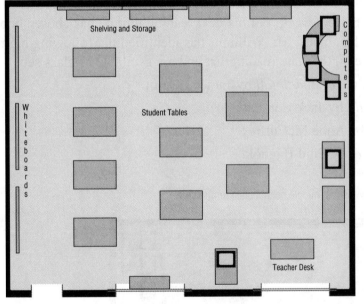

Ms. Heia's classroom regularly has four desktop computers connected to the school network for student use and a school-supplied teacher laptop for her personal use. She has also checked out an additional laptop computer and connected it to the school network, so that there are five student-use computers in her room (see Figure 4.4). Ms. Heia has decided to set up the circle roles and activities so that each discussion circle group has at least one member using technology on a regular basis. To do this she has selected two technology-enhanced roles (Vocabulary Elaborator and Graphic Organizer) to be part of the role set for each group. Each day that the discussion circle meets, the students advance one position. This way, each time the group meets, one or two members will be using technology to complete their roles while the other members are using nontech resources. Students will change roles as often as the teacher feel appropriate. Ms. Heia has also coordinated with the library media specialist so that if more computer access is needed, students can use some of the library media center computers to assist them with their roles. The roles that Ms. Heia has selected for this literature circle are:

1. Discussion Coordinator
2. Vocabulary Elaborator
3. Literary Expositor
4. Graphic Illustrator
5. Background Researcher
6. Graphic Organizer
7. Connector
8. Mapper/Tracker

Middle School: Living with Animals

Mr. Williams teaches reading in a rural middle school. His average class size is about 30 students in each period. Currently his school is also working to extend the class time for language and math and has developed a form of block scheduling for those two areas. This means that Mr. Williams has classes for double periods twice a week. For his next reading unit he has chosen books about living with animals. Mr. Williams has identified the following high-interest books which are on the state reading list and are available as class sets:

- *All Creatures Great and Small* by James Herriot
- *Call of the Wild* by Jack London
- *Dragonsong* by Anne McCaffrey
- *National Velvet* by Enid Bagnold

Figure 4.5 Mr. Williams' middle school classroom setup.

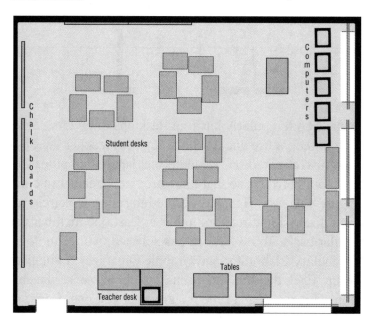

- *Old Yeller* by Fred Gipson
- *Tarzan* by Edgar Rice Burroughs

Single copies of the books are made available in the class for students to use to make their reading choices. Students write a list of their three favorites in order of choice and turn in the list to Mr. Williams. He collects the students' choices and uses them to create six reading groups of five students each. Mr. Williams' plans to have students read their books for homework and as part of the extended reading time during the block of scheduled classes. Two of the books (*Tarzan* and *Call of the Wild*) are available as free eBooks, so he also plans to work with the reading groups that choose these books to teach them about the additional reading scaffolds available, such as text-to-speech. Mr. Williams also plans to have the discussion groups meet weekly on Friday during the regular schedule day.

Mr. Williams' classroom regularly has five desktop computers connected to the school network for student use and a school-supplied teacher laptop for his personal use, which can also be used by students (see Figure 4.5). Additional laptop computers are available for checkout from the library media center if needed. Mr. Williams has decided to set up the circle roles and activities so that when each discussion circle meeting takes place, one of the circle groups will be fully technology enhanced, with each member of the group doing a technology-integrated activity. Each class session that the discussion circle meets, one of the student groups will move to the room's technology corner to work with the computers. Individual roles will be changed periodically with each group having the opportunity to participate with the technology-integrated roles. Using this method, each time the discussion circles meet on Friday, all the members of one circle will be using technology while the other five circles complete their roles using nontech resources. The roles that Mr. Williams has selected for this literature circle activity are as follows:

Table 4.3 Literature circle roles for nontech desk discussion circle and technology-based circle.

Desk circle	Tech circle
1. Discussion Coordinator	1. Web Researcher[tech]
2. Vocabulary Elaborator	2. Literary Expository[tech]
3. Literary Expository	3. Graphic Illustrator[tech]
4. Graphic Illustrator	4. Media hunter[tech]
5. Graphic Organizer	5. Graphic Organizer[tech]
6. Background Researcher	6. Mapper/Tracker[tech]
7. Connector	
8. Mapper/Tracker	

High School: Families in Isolation – Creating Community

Ms. Esperanza teaches language arts in a suburban high school. Her average class size is about 33 to 35 students in each period. For the next reading unit Ms. Esperanza has chosen a reading theme of families working together to create a community. She has identified the following books, which have a range of reading levels, that should be of high interest to her students, and are available as class sets:

- *Alas, Babylon* by Pat Frank
- *Anne Frank: The Diary of a Young Girl* by Anne Frank
- *The Day of the Triffids* by John Wyndham
- *The Swiss Family Robinson* by Johann Wyss

Single copies of the books are available in the class for students to use for making their reading choices. Ms. Esperanza polls students to find their choices and based on the polling creates seven reading groups of four or five students each. She plans to have the students read their books for homework, as part of the daily silent reading time, and have the literature circle meet weekly. A few of Ms. Esperanza's classes have a number of English as a second language (ESL, ELL, ESOL) students, some of whom are remedial readers. As a result, she is encouraging these students to group together to read *Swiss Family Robinson* so she can work closely with them, and because the book is freely available in electronic format in multiple versions, including one version written with single syllable words from the Blackmask (<http://www.blackmask.com>) library. The electronic book versions also can provide students additional reading scaffolds including text-to-speech and translating dictionaries.

Ms. Esperanza's classroom regularly has a set of four networked desktop computers for student use and her personal laptop. For this literature circle activity,

Figure 4.6 Ms. Esperanza's computer lab classroom setup.

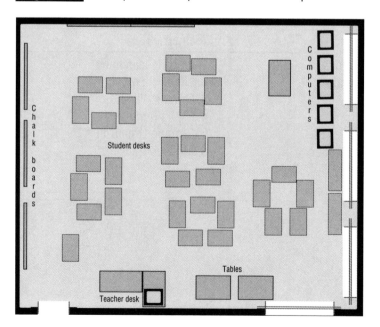

she has decided to have students participate with one-to-one computing and has signed up to have one of the three school computer labs for her class to use on a weekly basis for the next five weeks. This lab has 30 student workstations and a teacher station, which is connected to a video projector (see Figure 4.6). Six additional wireless laptop computers are available between the labs and will be set up for her classes. Ms. Esperanza has selected to have technology-enhanced circle roles for all students, so that when each literature circle meeting takes place, all students in her class will use technology as part of their process. Each member of the discussion circle will periodically advance through the list of technology-enhanced activities on a schedule that the teacher feels appropriate. The roles that Ms. Esperanza has selected for this literature circle activity are:

1. Vocabulary Elaborator
2. Background Researcher
3. Web Researcher
4. Graphic Illustrator
5. Graphic Organizer
6. Mapper/Tracker

Technology Resources

The following are examples of software (common or free) appropriate for student use with the different technology-integrated roles. Check the available computer for help or tutorial files for the different software applications or go to the online resources.

Audio Recording (*Literary Expositor*[(tech)])
Windows Sound Recorder (PC)
iTunes (MAC) <http://www.apple.com/itunes/>
Simple Sound (MAC)

Drawing (*Graphic Illustrator, Graphic Organizer*)
Windows Paint (PC)
Word Processor drawing tools

Desktop Publishing (*Graphic Illustrator, Graphic Organizer*)
MS Word (PC/MAC)
Windows WordPad (PC)
TextEdit (MAC)
SimpleText (MAC)
TexEdit (MAC) <http://www.tex-edit.com/>
AppleWorks (PC/MAC) <http://www.apple.com/appleworks/>

Web Browsing (*Vocabulary Elaborator, Graphic Illustrator, Graphic Organizer, Background Researcher, Media Hunter, Web Researcher, Mapper/Tracker*)
Internet Explorer (PC/MAC) <http://www.microsoft.com/downloads>
FireFox (PC/MAC) <http://www.firefox.com/>

Concept Mapping *(Graphic Organizer)*

Inspiration <http://www.inspiration.com> (PC/Mac)
Award-winning concept map software that can incorporate images and read aloud.

CmapTools <http://cmap.ihmc.us/Index.html> (PC/Mac)
Cmap is concept-mapping software available to schools at no cost.

Some additional online research and reference resources that can be used by students include:

Awesome Library <http://www.awesomelibrary.org>
Organizes the Web with 15,000 carefully reviewed resources, including the top five percent in education.

BookRags <http://www.bookrags.com/index.html>
Book notes and over 1,500 novels (HTML) available.

Britannica.com <http://www.britannica.com>
Users can simultaneously search the world's most respected encyclopedia.

CIA World Fact Book
<http://www.cia.gov/cia/publications/factbook/index.html>
An HTML-based book about every country in the world.

Electric Library <http://www.elibrary.com>
Full-text documents and images from magazines, maps, books and reports, newspapers and newswires, radio, TV and government transcripts, and pictures.

ElectricLibrary's Encyclopedia.com <http://www.encyclopedia.com>
More than 14,000 free articles from *The Concise Columbia Electronic Encyclopedia* (3rd ed.).

Encyclopedia Smithsonian <http://www.si.edu/resource/faq>
A resource for teachers and students with thousands of sources on hundreds of topics.

Information Please <http://www.infoplease.com>
Offers online almanacs, encyclopedias, and dictionaries (links under "Sources").

The Internet Public Library <http://www.ipl.org>
A resource for a variety of collections.

Library Spot <http://www.libraryspot.com>
A free virtual library resource center for educators and students, library media specialists and their patrons, families, businesses, and just about anyone exploring the Web for valuable research information.

SparkNotes <http://www.sparknotes.com/>
From Barnes & Noble, *SparkNotes* (like *Cliff Notes*) offers help in understanding literature free online.

The U.S. Library of Congress <http://www.loc.gov>
Comprised of approximately 115 million items in virtually all formats, languages, and subjects, this Web site is the Internet location of the largest library in the world.

Wikipedia <http://en.wikipedia.org/wiki/Main_Page>

A Web-based, multi-language encyclopedia written collaboratively by volunteers all over the world; contains entries both on traditional encyclopedic topics and on almanac, gazetteer, and current events topics. As of this writing *Wikipedia* had over 1.6 million articles.

Integrating technology into literature circle activities can be effectively accomplished in a wide variety of class technology settings. The lack of one-to-one computing in the classroom, where every student has a computer, does not mean a teacher can't integrate some technology-enhanced activities. Today's student lives in a technology-enhanced world, and it is important to integrate the new literacies, which include technology, into class activities. This chapter helped identify for educators some of the strategies and applications they can use to integrate technology into literature circles. Consider starting with one or two technology roles for students and expand that as opportunities and interest occur.

References

Cavanaugh, Cathy. *Clips from the Classroom: Learning with Technology*. Upper Saddle River, NJ: Prentice Hall (2005).

IRA (International Reading Association). "Integrating Literacy and Technology in the Curriculum: A position statement." *International Reading Association*. Newark, Delaware (2002).

ISTE (International Society for Technology in Education). "National Educational Technology Standards for Students: Technology Foundation Standards for All Students." *International Society for Technology in Education* (2000). Retrieved August 2005 from <http://cnets.iste.org/students/s_stands.html>.

Kamil, Michael. "Adolescents and Literacy: Reading for the 21st Century." *Alliance for Excellent Education* (2003). Retrieved April 2005 from <http://www.all4ed.org/publications/AdolescentsAndLiteracy.pdf>.

Kress, Gunther. *Literacy in the New Media Age*. London: Routledge (2003).

Lamb, Annette, Nancy R. Smith, and Larry Johnson. "Themes and Literature Circles." *eduScapes* (1999, updated 02/03). Retrieved September 2004 from <http://eduscapes.com/ladders/themes/literacy.htm>.

Vocabulary Elaborator(tech)

Name: _____ Group: _____

Book: _____

Author: _____

Reading Assignment: page _____ to page_____

Assignment:

Your job is to develop a list of words for your group to define in the context of this book or part of this book. Your task is to help define these words from the reading and share with the others. The words you select to define should be words that you or other members of your group cannot pronounce, define, or understand in the way they are presented. To find your words:

1. First, point to the unexplained word and then underline or highlight it.

2. Next, read the sentence containing the unexplained word.

3. If you cannot comprehend the meaning of the word, read the preceding sentence to try to figure out the definition.

4. If you still don't have a definition for the marked word, read the next sentence after the marked word.

5. Lastly, use a dictionary to check the definition of the word. Use either an interactive dictionary that occurs when you highlight the word or visit an online dictionary site such as:

   - **The Internet Picture Dictionary** <http://www.pdictionary.com/>
   - **The Online Rhyming Dictionary** <http://www.writeexpress.com/online2.html>
   - **Different types of dictionaries** <http://directory.google.com/ Top/Kids_and_Teens/School_Time/Reference_Tools/Dictionaries/>
   - **Commonly-Used American Slang** <http://www.manythings.org/slang/>
   - **American Heritage Dictionary (online) – Bartleby** <http://www.bartleby.com/>

Usually dictionaries will give several meanings for a word, and it is important to look at each numbered definition and decide which one coincides with the marked word.

Words I have never heard before:
Words whose meaning I don't know:
Words I have seen before, but never used this way:

	Word	Page/Paragraph/Line	Definition
1			
2			
3			
4			
5			

Literary Expositor*(tech)*

Name: _____ Group: _____

Book: _____

Author: _____

Reading Assignment: page _____ to page_____

Assignment:

Your job is to select from the book or passage, by yourself or with help, several favorite or interesting passages. Your task is to select three or four of your favorite parts of the story to share aloud with your group members. As you read and find sections that you like, highlight the paragraphs and record the corresponding page numbers you enjoyed reading and want to hear read aloud. Possible reasons for selection include important, well written, humorous, informative, surprising, controversial, funny, confusing, and thought provoking.

Once you have selected your sentences, use a microphone and software (such as Windows Sound Recorder) to record your sentences into a computer and then play them back when having your discussion with the others. During the playing of the read-aloud segment, the other group members will play and listen intently to your recordings as they read along with the sections, determine and then share what particular aspect of the reading they enjoyed the most. After the book or section has been read in its entirety by the group, the reading clips can all be played or read aloud for review and to select which was the best overall. You must find at least three, but no more than five, sentences to read aloud to your group.

Page/Paragraph/Line	Reason	Sentence
1		
2		
3		
4		
5		

Graphic Illustrator^(tech)

Name: _____ Group: _____

Book: _____

Author: _____

Reading Assignment: page _____ to page_____

Assignment:

Your job is to draw two pictures using a paint or other drawing program on the computer that depict the main idea and feeling in the narrative. Your task is to create illustrations that show a character's interaction with other characters or story elements. After using the drawing tools to create your picture, add text labels to the parts to assist everyone with understanding your drawings. Also, after creating your pictures that show story or text ideas, you will discuss your idea pictures with your group. You might want to print out a copy of your picture to share with your group. Once you have drawn your pictures, add to your picture by creating a text box and write out a description of the characters' interaction in complete sentences and standard paragraph form. Use the space below to develop your paragraph drafts.

Draft Paragraph Descriptions:_____

Graphic Organizer^(tech)

Name: _____ Group: _____

Book: _____

Author: _____

Reading Assignment: page _____ to page_____

Assignment:

Your job is to create a content or concept map from the reading that helps your group better understand the reading. Create your concept map from the reading with the main idea at the center or top and the related ideas moving out with descriptors connecting verbs. You can create it with mind mapping software, such as Inspiration or Cmap Tools. You can also use other digital concept mapping tools and resources (many tools are available online) to create maps such as a Venn diagram, timeline, or concept web. Print your concept map to share with the other group members and see if they have any other points or connections to add. You can make any type of graphic organizer you wish, or choose from the options available from one of the sites listed below.

- **International Reading Association's Read•Write•Think**
  <http://www.readwritethink.org/student_mat/index.asp>

- **Teach-nology Web site**
  <http://www.teach-nology.com/worksheets/graphic/>

- **Education World Templates (doc)**
  <http://www.educationworld.com/tools_templates/>

Character Map | Timeline | Character Interaction | Story Line/Plot | Compare & Contrast (Venn)

Background Researcher _(tech)_

Name: _____ Group: _____

Book: _____

Author: _____

Reading Assignment: page _____ to page _____

Assignment:

Your job is to read and identify from the text when and where the writing occurred. Your task is to identify the historical time frame or location and research a topic of your choice related to that time or location. In the text, characters behave in a certain manner, or events are described in a certain way, which reflects a specific period in time or location. This is known as the setting. You should investigate a topic of interest that happened in that specific time period or location of the setting. If the book is not story based, identify a fact from the reading and research that fact and find something of interest to you. From the readings, using the space below, identify at least three statements that indicate the historical or locational (or factual) setting. Then go online and find an associated Web site that you find interesting concerning that time or location. Share your findings and Web sites with your group members during the discussion. Give the URL, describe the site and how it relates to the reading, and explain why you found it interesting.

Setting Statements:

Page/Paragraph/Line	Year/Location	Sentence
1		
2		
3		

Interesting Web Site Findings:
URL – Title – Description – Interest

_____

_____

_____

_____

_____

_____

_____

_____

Media Hunter(tech)

Name: _____ Group: _____

Book: _____

Author: _____

Reading Assignment: page _____ to page _____

Assignment:

Your job is to read and identify from the text interesting aspects included in the text and then locate associated media to share with the other literature circle group members. Your task is to identify some aspect from the reading and then search and find either images, sound files, or video related to that topic, time, or location. You can search to find media on a topic of interest that happened in that specific time period or location of the setting. If the book is not story based, identify a fact from the reading and search for associated media concerning that fact. In the list below, identify from the readings at least three statements that indicate the historical or locational (or factual) setting. Then go online and use media search tools to find associated images, sound files, or videos from Web sites. You can use the media search tools listed below or others you may know. These media files should be ones that you find interesting concerning that fact, time, or location. Share your findings and their Web sites' URLs by either copying and pasting the images into a document and printing it or by playing sound or video files with your discussion members. Make sure you explain to your group members how the media relates to the reading and be sure to give the source URL.

Search tools:

- **Google Image Search** <http://images.google.com/>
- **Lycos Multimedia Search** <http://multimedia.lycos.com/>
- **Search Engine Watch listing of media search engines**
  <http://searchenginewatch.com/links/article.php/2156251>
- **National Archives media tools**
  <http://www.archives.gov/research_room/research_paths.html>

Page/Paragraph/Line	Location Statement
1	
2	
3	

Media Web Sites Findings:

URL – Format – Description – Relation

Web Researcher $^{(tech)}$

Name: _____   Group: _____

Book: _____

Author: _____

Reading Assignment: page _____ to page_____

Assignment:

Your job concerns a study of either the book or the author. With this role you create a summary book study or author study from the material you read, and construct a question you would like answered by the author (or another expert). If you decide to do a book study, then you would be looking at reviews or resources related to the book or its contents. Search for the book title and then review your results. If you have decided to do an author study, you will be looking for information and biographical data about the author such as who he is, what else has he written, when did he start writing, what else is he working on now, where is he from, when was he born. One way to start getting information on the book or author is to go to Amazon.com and search for the book. There you will find the start of some reviews and a link to the author's name. If you click on the name link, it should also produce a list of other books by that author currently for sale from Amazon. Don't think that one site is all you will need to visit. Find out if the author has a site. Look for a publisher site that may give you insight and information about the book or author. Find your sites and information, then copy and paste relevant portions into a word processor (don't forget to get the reference and URL), then combine your findings into a new summary. Share your summary book or author study with your group. Now with your group, develop a question that you would like to ask the author of the book about the material. If your author or topic (expert) is not available from the list below, use a search engine with *ask author* and the author's name, or *ask expert* and the topic name as the keyword search terms. Many times authors are available to ask questions through e-mail. Consider asking an author or other expert your question (with teacher permission). When you get an answer, be sure to share it with your group and class.

- **Ask an Author** <http://www.ipl.org/div/kidspace/askauthors/AuthorLinks.html>
- **Ask an Expert** <http://www.cln.org/int_expert.html>
- **Ask Dr. Science** <http://www.drscience.com/>
- **Ask Dr. Universe** <http://www.wsu.edu/DrUniverse/Contents.html>
- **Children's Literature Web Guide** <http://www.ucalgary.ca/~dkbrown/>
- **CLN Ask an Expert** <http://www.cln.org/int_expert.html>
- **ExpertCentral** <http://www.expertcentral.com>
- **Internet Public Library's Literary Criticism** <http://www.ipl.org/div/litcrit/>
- **Scientific American – Ask the Experts** <http://www.sciam.com/askexpert_directory.cfm>

Our Question:_____

_____

Mapper/Tracker*(tech)*

Name: _____   Group: _____

Book: _____

Author: _____

Reading Assignment: page _____ to page_____

Assignment:

Your job concerns the book's characters or content and the location. You will create some form of map representation of the reading content. The map can be a tracking map, a comparison map, collage or series of location maps. The question you are trying to answer is where is the content from the reading occurring? A **tracking map** is one that provides a visual display that follows or shows in order where events took place. A **comparison map** is one that shows your actual location relative to the material in the reading. The **map collage** contains a collection of various maps of locations presented in the reading. In each case you should edit the maps, such as adding marks onto the map image to specify location. Start by finding location information from the reading, noting where it occurs in the text and the locations that the text is describing. Now make your map. One way this can be done is to copy the map into a drawing or paint program and use the tools to add marks, or waypoints, trackways, and character or event names onto the map to identify the reading location or locations. Once you have completed your map or maps, write a descriptive paragraph that explains your map materials.

What type of map are you creating?   ☐ Tracking   ☐ Comparison   ☐ Collage

- **CIA World FactBook** <http://www.cia.gov/cia/publications/factbook/index.html>
- **Yahoo Maps** <http://maps.yahoo.com/>
- **Google Maps** <http://maps.google.com/>
- **Mapquest** <http://www.mapquest.com/>
- **Microsoft TerraServer** <http://terraserver.microsoft.com/>

Location notes

Page/Paragraph/Line	Location Statement
1	
2	
3	

Map Description: _____

_____

_____

Digital Logs, Journals, and Discussions

The American Association of School Librarians (AASL) Information Literacy Standards addressed in this chapter:

- Information Literacy: 1
- Independent Learning: 4
- Social Responsibility: 7, 8, and 9

The International Society for Technology in Education (ISTE) Technology Foundation Standards for All Students addressed in this chapter:

- Basic operations and concepts: 1.1 and 1.2
- Technology productivity tools: 3.1 and 3.2
- Technology communications tools: 4.1 and 4.2
- Technology research tools: 5.2
- Technology problem-solving and decision-making tools: 6.2

For more information on these standards, see page ix.

This chapter will examine the application of telecollaboration technology and how it can be used by students for independent or interactive reading journal or log applications, expanding the discussion group beyond the classroom. The online collaborative tools can also be used to create an online Socratic discussion. Online logs and journals can be used by a single student, a few students, or even a whole class depending on the needs of the students and the availability of the technology. A listing of online discussion and journaling resources is included at the end of this chapter.

Reading Logs and Journaling

For many teachers, student reading logs or journals are a standard classroom activity associated with reading. These journals or logs can be incorporated into the discussion circle or completed as a separate activity. Using digital meeting spaces for students to record their log and have discussions allows students to meet and interact in, what to them, may be a familiar environment, using technology to which they are both attracted and comfortable. Here students can talk about what they read and understand, what they don't understand, what they agree with, or don't, and their questions. Journaling is quite different from a literature circle, in which the student has a specific role or activity and interacts with other students from the discussion group in person. The digital reading log or journal asks students to record their thoughts for themselves, posting information for others, or interacting with others in an online environment, and results in shifting the "communication" to the far right on the communication continuum (See Figure 5.1).

Figure 5.1 Enhancing the communication dimensions by using technology such as blogs, wikis, and online forums.

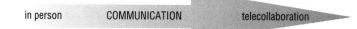

in person   COMMUNICATION   telecollaboration

Enhancing Logs and Journals with Technology

Jeff Wilhelm (2000), when discussing Bolter's research, suggests that "…if our students are not reading and composing with various electronic technologies, then they are illiterate…right now…" (4). Having students incorporate technology into journaling is not a difficult proposal. Today's students have lived their whole lives in the information age. A good number of students will need no instruction about these methods of communication technology, and instead could teach us. If you asked them to tell you the price of a stamp today, you likely wouldn't find many students who could tell you the correct price, but they can discuss at length communicating with text messaging, e-mail, and chat or discussion rooms.

The use of an online journal or log can provide students with an expanded experience. Such an activity can connect two or more groups of students, such as upper and lower grades, classes from different schools, and students from different parts of the world. Together these different students can progress together and share opinions about issues that are important to them. Students can also use these online communication applications for discussion with practicing professionals and experts. For example, a student reading from a book can join an author's discussion group and interact with the author and other people interested in the author's writing. By contributing to the virtual discussion, a student can become a contributing member to a larger group, sharing his or her insight while using today's communication skills. Through journals and logs, students can find others who share interests in what they are reading for discussion, even if they can't find anyone in class for discussion.

Students have a variety of online applications with which they can conduct their own digital journals or discussions. Some of the online applications include discussion forums, Web logs or blogs, and wikis. Each of these applications allows a student to participate by writing with a tool that is published online. An option with a number of these tools is that a student can set the information to be private or public.

Research has found that students' participation in online writing activities develops communication skills through participation in "written conversation" (Kamil 2003). Because students must communicate with each other through reading and writing in a computer-mediated environment, there is an increased demand on literacy skills. As there is no supplement to the written text such as intonation, gestures or facial expressions, students must rely on only the use of words and symbols to make their communications understood. Kamil (2003), in reporting on research findings of the effects of computer communications on reading and writing, stated that students' written communications were found to improve in quality. These technologies, therefore, have been found to be effective and motivating to many students and are often part of their lives outside school. They are environments where students often feel comfortable and where many students who might be too shy to participate in a face-to-face situation can participate comfortably (Beach and Lundell 1998).

> An **Internet forum** is an interactive Web application that provides areas for discussion, which can be either threaded or non-threaded. Internet forums are also commonly known as Web forums, message boards, discussion boards, discussion groups, or simply forums.
>
> A **Blog** or **Weblog** is a Web-based application for publication of information in chronological order, with individual blog entries date and time stamped, usually with new entries at the top of the Web page. Blogs exist in a wide range of topics and can usually be set to allow visitors to leave comments.
>
> A **Wiki** is a collaborative Web software application that allows visitors to actually add content or edit a Web page. A **Wiki farm** is a wiki hosting service that uses online servers.

New Log and Journaling Tools

New communication tools such as blogs, wikis, and forums have changed the basic process of putting information on the Web by making interactive tools available to everyone. Before the development of these discussion tools, information put onto the Internet went one way: someone with technical ability put it up and people could use it. Now students with basic computer skills and Internet access can create and interact in a sophisticated Web space within minutes (Colgan 2005). A Pew

Internet & American Life Project report stated that seven percent of adult Internet users in the U.S. have created blogs (Lenhart, A., Horrigan, J., and Fallows, D. 2004), with overall blog readership up 58% in one year. Teens are estimated to be approximately half of all blog creators. While many students are using blogs and other forms of interactive communication tools on the Internet to socialize, the potential exists for using them in classrooms as productive, high-interest, collaborative tools for learning (see Figure 5.2).

Figure 5.2   Planet Book Club's Classroom Connection in the Kids section at <http://www.planetbookclub.com/>.

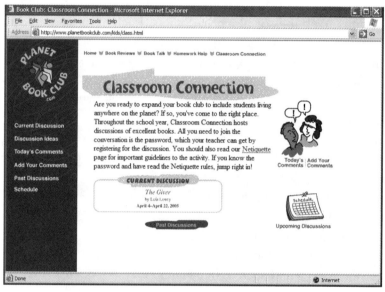

Technology-enhanced learning activities can be used by students interacting with each other in an online communication environment. Using this kind of technology makes it possible for students who are in different classes or grade levels to interact with each other about a reading topic, either in real time or asynchronously (more on this topic in Chapter 6). A student can read a passage from a text and then compose questions or comments to be posted for the next student to read and respond to, even if the next student attends class at a different time. This online discussion format can be expanded beyond the local area to include readers who may be miles or continents away. Such a long distance literature or Socratic circle can require readers to make comments about a book in the blog or discussion forum, and then other members can post comments to the blog or discussion, or e-mail comments to specific members of their discussion group. These online tools can also be used by individual readers, much like a personal reading journal or log. Students can create their own online journals and logs and either keep them personal or open their writing to the public at large.

Personal Reading Journals or Logs

A number of different kinds of reading journals or logs are commonly used in classrooms today. Usually a reading log is a notebook where students can react to what they have read. They may write about how they feel, insight they gained, or what they did concerning their reading. For example, they may write about the plot, characters, setting, or writing style. The purpose of the reading log is to provide a framework for students to develop or enhance critical-thinking abilities and to provide documentation for the teacher. Some common types of reading logs include:

- **Response Logs** – Students think critically about events and learning experiences that have occurred in the reading and record those thoughts, or they record their own personal experiences or connections to the text. With a response log, students demonstrate their ability to interpret meaning from text as they transition from reading into writing in their own words.

- **Explanation and Process Logs** – Students organize steps sequentially with written explanations or processes. These logs are generally used with topics like mathematics and science, where the reading involves a specific process or a series of steps. One goal of this kind of log is for students to demonstrate the ability to follow or give directions.

- **Perspective Log** – Students make connections and judgments based on different points of view. Students look at the situation from different perspectives and communicate their feelings and ideas.

All of these types of student writing can be facilitated using an online reading journal or log. Students can create their own personal reading log by joining a service such as Kidspoint (<http://www.kidspoint.org/>) (see Figure 5.3), or by having a school-based blog or wiki tool for students to use. Students can be directed to include specific tasks such as "include a summary, in 150 words or less, of the material you have read," or "write a prediction about what you think will happen next," in addition to developing their own reading log.

Figure 5.3   Kidspoint's personal online reading log, available at <http://www.kidspoint.org/>, Central Rappahannock Regional Library, Fredericksburg, VA.

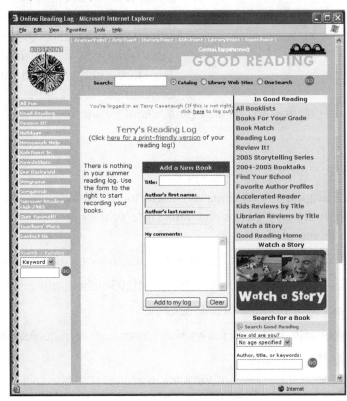

Booktalks

Figure 5.4 Sample booktalks on *Artemis Fowl* at Nancy Keane's Booktalk site at <http://nancykeane.com/booktalks/>.

Normally a booktalk involves a teacher or a library media specialist giving a brief talk about a particular book to generate interest in the book. Booktalks can be used to introduce students to a book, or as an activity from the literature circle, where the student or discussion group creates a booktalk. An online booktalk is similar to a presented one, but in a written format. Nancy Keane (2005) uses the analogy that a booktalk is like a movie trailer. The objective of a booktalk is to generate interest by giving a future reader some information about elements such as plot and characters, without giving away the ending. A booktalk is not supposed to be a book summary, an analysis, or a book review. Writing a booktalk is similar to writing the back cover of a paperback novel. It can include quoted passages, character information, and hints about what will happen, all in a short quick reading format. Students can submit their booktalks to book discussion sites, such Nancy Keane's Booktalks (<http://nancykeane.com/booktalks/>) (see Figure 5.4), or to a blogging site, such as one that was created for a school by a teacher or a library media specialist.

A few online booktalk resources and examples:

Apple Education Language Arts (look at Short Story Commercials and Book Ads) <http://education.apple.com/education/ilife/subject_template.php?subject_id=2>

Book Talk using iMovie <http://www.users.ties.k12.mn.us/~wbierden/booktalk.htm>

Booktalking Basics <http://www.albany.edu/%7edj2930/aboutbt.html>

Digital Booktalks <http://digitalbooktalk.ucf.edu/>

Drs. Cavanaugh Booktalk Tech <http://www.drscavanaugh.org/ebooks/booktalk/>

HarperCollins's Author's Notes <http://www.harpercollins.com/authornotes.asp?page=notes>

Joni Richards Bodart's The Booktalker <http://www.thebooktalker.com/>

Kenton County Public Library Staff Booktalks
<http://www.kenton.lib.ky.us/videos/booktalks/>

Nancy Keane's Booktalks – Quick and Simple <http://nancykeane.com/booktalks/>

Prairie Middle Students Video Booktalks
<http://www.prairiepride.org/teachertools/ViewAssignment.php?AssignID=1 9589&SylID=327>

Promoting Reading with Booktalks: <http://www.eddept.wa.edu.au/cip/learntech/eng/pr/>

Teachers@Random <http://www.randomhouse.com/teachers/librarians/booktalks.html>

Yahoo Discussion Group: Booktalkers <http://groups.yahoo.com/group/booktalkers>

Book Discussions

People interacting and "talking" about a book can occur in an online book discussion community. A book discussion usually involves analysis of a book. In a book discussion, students post information or their feelings or thoughts, so others can read and respond to them, creating a two-way (or more) dialog about the book. These discussions can take place in an online forum (see Figure 5.5), a

Figure 5.5 Book discussion forums on different books at the ePALS Book Club Talk <http://www.epals.com/projects/book_club/>.

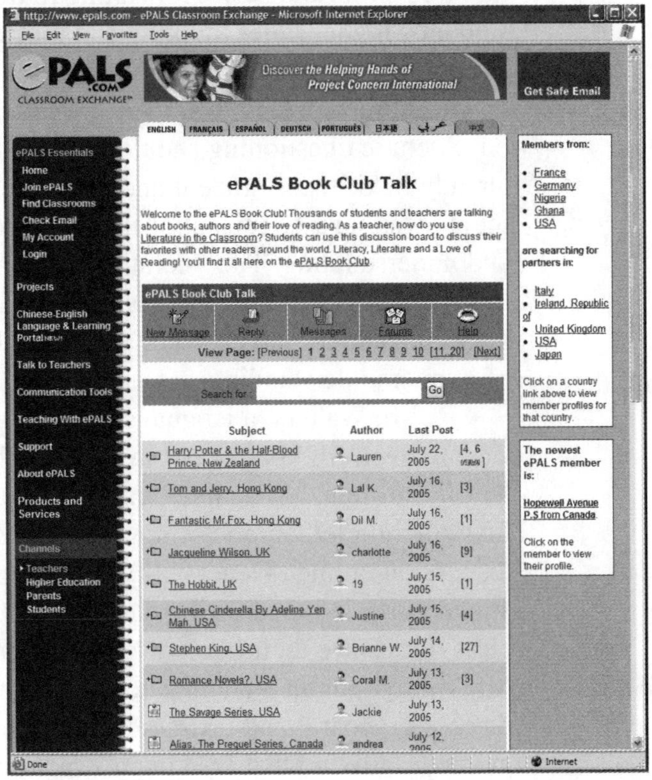

Figure 5.6 Book discussion on *Holes* by Louis Sachar at the Blogger Book Club of the Roselle Public Library District, Roselle, IL, <http://www.roselle.lib.il.us/YouthServices/bookclub/bookclub.htm>.

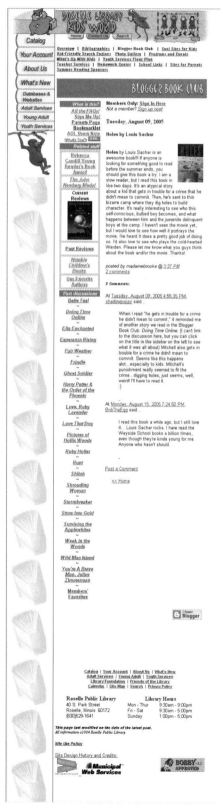

chat room, or even a reading blog (see Figure 5.6). Here students' writings are stored for others to read, usually in a time posted or threaded topic display. Blogs are usually time based, with the most recent post being at the top. Discussion boards are usually threaded, meaning the discussion starter is at the top, with listed replies below and to the right in an outline form.

For more information and resources for book discussions, see Chapter 2's Book Discussion Guides.

Digital Socratic Literature Circle

If the teacher is organizing a class to use a blog for an interactive discussion, then the online discussion can become the medium for a Socratic discussion. In Socratic discussions, students are divided into two groups that discuss the text and discuss the discussion. Lesley Lambright (1995), in the article "Creating Dialog: Socratic Seminars and Educational Reform," states that Socratic Literature Circles (Seminars) are where "exploratory intellectual conversation centered on a text" (30) occurs. The goal of the Socratic literature circle goes beyond the lower order thinking skills and surface meaning to develop students' higher order thinking and metacognitive skills. The students develop the process of how one question can lead to further questions, and so on. Socratic questioning should identify the ideas already held by the student and make students more aware and cognizant of their own learning and understanding. The Socratic questioning method is a systematic process for examining ideas, questions, and answers that form the basis of human understanding.

Mr. Walters, a language arts teacher at Cedar Creek Middle School in Youngsville, North Carolina, has adapted in his class a literature circle/Socratic seminar for the students' discussion online (Walters 2003). While students attend class and read the books as part of their class, they have their book discussions online. Mr. Walters set up a reading schedule, an online discussion board, and text-associated seminar guides. He found that creating a structured environment for the discussion provided for better work and accountability by students. While some of the final results for his small class were mixed, he found that "most of the students did make comments, and many replied thoughtfully to other students' comments" (Walters 2003 Socratic Seminar Success). He also found that most of the comments were reader-response based and on task.

The standard structure or rules of a Socratic literature circle relate to what is read, how the students are physically arranged, and students' interaction procedures. Student discussion focuses on a short passage of text, which should be read critically. In an in-person group, the students are physically arranged in two concentric circles. Students in the interior circle explore and find meaning from the text that is read. Students in the exterior circle are observers and at this time do not interact with the members of the inner circle. After a specified amount of time, or when the discussion has ended, the outer circle provides feedback about the inner circle's discussion. For the next passage the two circles change places and roles, and then the process is repeated.

In an online Socratic literature circle there are still two groups, but they do not physically meet together. The inner circle students are "posters," who discuss the section of reading by posting their thoughts and questions. The outer circle students are discussion "lurkers," hovering in the background, reading what is posted without contributing to the discussion that is occurring. Then after the first part of the discussion has ended, the lurkers become active posters, providing feedback and questions concerning the first discussion. Then the roles switch, with the previous lurkers becoming the active posters, and the old posters now lurking.

Classroom Models

There are a number of ways that digital logging or journaling can be incorporated into the classroom as part of a reading activity's discussion (see Figure 5.7). One way would be for an *Individual*, such as individual class members, to use online journaling resources or Web sites to record their own thoughts and feelings concerning what was read for either themselves or to bring to their discussion circle. Most systems will provide a choice whether to keep the information private or to share it with others. An example of the individual case would be a student posting to his or her own blog, to create an online reading journal. Another case is the *Within Class* situation, in which multiple class members participate together in an online discussion, extending the circle's discussion time beyond the class period. Some

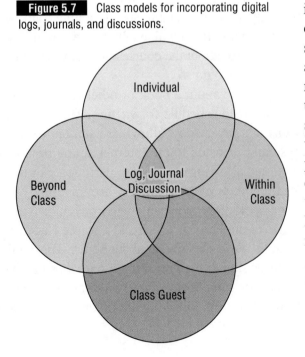

Figure 5.7 Class models for incorporating digital logs, journals, and discussions.

Students who are posting to book clubs, booktalks, or blogs usually use a text box or form where submissions are written. Most of these tools do not include writing support such as spell check. Students who desire such support can write their posting first using a word processor such as MS Word, or use an online tool such as the Google Toolbar. The 2005 version of the Google Toolbar included a tool button titled **"Check"** which is used to check spelling when typing into Web forms. After writing into the online form, the user just presses the toolbar's spell check button to check the text in the box. Misspelled or unknown words are underlined and in red (see Figure 5.8). Clicking on a marked word produces a selection of possible word spellings. The word can also be ignored or added to a personal spelling dictionary. The Google Toolbar is available free from Google at <http://www.google.com/>. Look in the "more" section.

within class examples are an interactive blog with students responding to each other's postings, or a wiki that students use to cooperatively construct information that they wish to share. In the case of *Beyond Class*, individual class members participate with others outside of class such as by posting to an online booktalk or by joining others interested in the topic in a forum discussion. This format also allows a literature circle group to consist of members from more than a single class or school. The last format is the *Class Guest*, in which outside members are able to join in and participate with class members. For example, students who are homeschooled, hospitalized, homebound, or in another school, or an adult guest such as a subject matter expert or an author, can join with a class to participate in an online forum discussion or respond to a class blog.

It is important to integrate these technology-enhanced forms of writing into the students' course, so that students understand there is a value to their participation online in the classroom. What students write can be class assessments, which can take place during class or as part of homework. Students can turn in printouts of their postings or instructors can request that students submit links, so that instructors can read what students have written. Using this material, teachers can assess the work for content as well as check for inappropriate participation. A good plan is to set up a posting schedule, so students know by when they should be posting, such as weekly or biweekly. It is important to specify a time frame or deadline for the initial posting or response to an online talk. Make sure that students are required to participate regularly throughout the course and that time and technology are made available for them to do so.

An advantage of writing online about a book or other reading is that students can set their own personalized schedule for writing. These sites are available at all times of day or night, every day, allowing a student to write when they feel ready. Such writings can be posted to the Internet at any time from any place, with the proper connections, allowing students to participate during the summer, when they are sick at home, or even when they are traveling.

Participation in an online book discussion can range from an activity for individual students as an alternate or enrichment activity, to a whole class activity in which all students in a class visit the Web sites to talk about books. This kind of activity can have excellent results as students are selecting discussions in which they want to participate based on a topic or genre that is already interesting to them. For example, students who like Harry Potter can join a discussion on the latest book or one of the previous volumes.

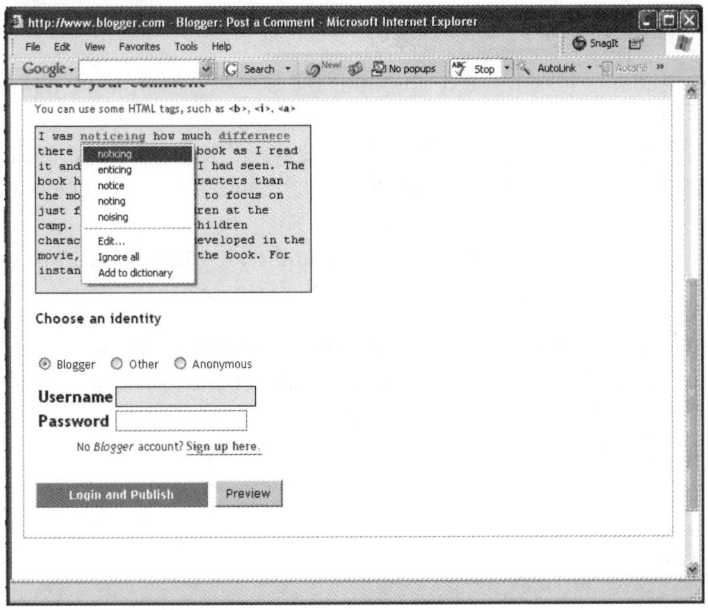

Figure 5.8 Using the Google Toolbar to check spelling in a posting form.

Educator's Role

To better prepare students to participate in these online discussions, the educator should perform some of the activities with the students. First prepare students in advance by setting up a practice forum or blog, then instruct them on how to participate. As part of this instruction, the instructor should demonstrate common practices such as login and posting, and then assist students who have problems with technical ability or computer access. Educators should model a positive tone in the writings and demonstrate respectful participation. If students are participating in a class or in the library media center, it is important to monitor their participation, but also to have a minimal presence so as not to control, dominate, or inhibit student expression. Show students the value and benefits of communication and collaboration as it can occur online. Instructors should nurture students' expression of ideas, perhaps by recapping what some students have submitted, referring to their responses, or even questioning them on their posted thoughts.

Technology Management

Using online journaling in the classroom requires that students have either handheld devices or access to computers in order to access the journaling sites. It is possible to have successful experiences with online journaling in a variety of classroom configurations, from the one-computer classroom to the full computer lab. (See Chapter 4 for more details and strategies concerning classroom configurations and management.)

Table 5.1 Class designs and technology applications for technology-enhanced circles.

Class Design	Strategies
One-computer class centers or two-to-few computers	■ Students take turns throughout the day or class period as they have free time. ■ Post a schedule of times when a student will enter and read journals. ■ Use the "passport" to identify which students need access to the computers. ■ Use a slider with student names and slide the names from the "not yet" side to the "been there" side.
Whole class or one-to-one computing	■ All one-computer and two-to-few activities above, plus: Whole class reading and responding activitiy. All students in a class post and read as a class activity. ■ Journaling is part of start/warm-up activity.

Educator Collaboration

Having students participate in an interactive online environment to discuss books can provide an excellent opportunity for collaboration between teachers, library media specialists, and other school instructors. Consider creating connections between individual teachers and computer or lab teachers to set up room switching so that whole classes can participate in the online journaling environment. Another option is for all students in a grade or on a team who take a computing class to participate in an online discussion or book club as an activity for that course.

Library media specialists can be excellent resources to assist students and classes in going online for discussions. They can work with classes to inform teachers and students of options available for online discussions, journals, and booktalks. Local library media specialists can work with regional technology trainers to provide in-service to teachers and training to students concerning online discussions on topics such as netiquette. Library media specialists can collaborate with teachers to find and post appropriate high-interest blog and discussion sites for students. These sites can be posted to a Web page on the school or library media center site that directs students to wide range of high-interest books sites which students can join for discussion.

The library media center can also be adapted to encourage online book discussion. Posters placed throughout the school can let students know about discussion sites that they can join. Library media specialists can identify computers within the library media center as places where students can independently work on projects such as digital journaling and book blogs (see Figure 5.9). At the specified computers, they can place flyers or card sets to provide instruction and encourage students to join a book discussion. Library media specialists can also list and describe recommended book discussion sites in the library media center section of the school news.

Benefits of Online Journals and Discussions

Online discussions and journals can also provide benefits to participating classes and students. First, this form of communication can greatly extend the classroom learning by allowing remote participants to take part, while having students use the tools and skills they have learned in a public forum. In many ways, by occurring online, the learning has become more individualized. Students' responses to a topic are not limited in time or length, because students have the opportunity and freedom to continue dialogues about topics that are of interest to them. This form of discussion or journal also can promote a more democratic exchange between participating members. In any class of 25 to 30 students, there will be dominant personalities and students who may feel intimidated or unmotivated to speak. Therefore discussions, even in small groups, do not allow equal time to all students. In the online medium, each student has a voice that can be heard and documented by anyone who chooses to read his or her comments. For the teacher, this online format offers the advantage of archiving and documenting the student journals and discussions, which can then be used as assessment items. The online format also allows students more time to formulate their responses and opinions, because students have the flexibility to add their input when they are prepared. Some students will choose to answer questions immediately, while others prefer to consider the responses of others first. This experience allows students to participate in a professional communication process of today, gaining technology experience, and meeting technology and communication standards.

These forms of online activities are creative, constructive, and encourage critical thinking as the student writes. This form of writing is very open-ended and encourages students to present information and take positions on what they have read. Responding to a topic usually requires organized thoughts and a synthesis of the concepts or content of the reading.

Sample Online Book Clubs, Logs, and Discussions that Students Can Join

Adbooks

<http://www.adbooks.org/>

An e-mail list that can be subscribed to for discussing young adult literature, designed for people of all ages.

African American Literature Book Club

<http://aalbc.com/>

Includes discussion boards, book reviews, and author profiles.

Book BackChat

<http://english.unitecnology.ac.nz/bookchat/home.php>

Book BackChat has online discussions about books, each term discussing about five books. While the BackChats usually involve New Zealand schools, other schools and students from other countries are welcome.

BookBlog

<http://www.bookblog.net/>

BookBlog features online book clubs and discussions about popular literature with different books each month.

BookTalk

<http://www.booktalk.org/>

BookTalk is an online book discussion community dedicated to the advancement of critical thinking, with regularly scheduled online chats with authors.

Chatelaine Forums

<http://www.chatelaine.com/applications/forums/fserver-jsp/2/>

This site is a general book discussion forum hosted by the Canadian women's magazine.

Classic Reading Group

<http://groups.yahoo.com/group/classicsreadinggroup/>

This Yahoo! group reads and discusses one classic literary work that changes each month.

ePals Book Club

<http://www.epals.com/projects/book_club/>

Teachers can find other teachers to be club partners and student can post their own book reviews and discuss books on this site.

Global Book Club

<http://www.ncsu.edu/globalbookclub/>

The purpose of this site is to highlight and share three outstanding Young Adult novels each month. The site provides numerous novel-by-novel activities for classes and will share submitted projects. The site can also be used to establish electronic dialogue journals between students.

Kidspoint

<http://www.kidspoint.org/good_reading/reading_log.asp>

This site provides an online reading log to record thoughts on books that are being read.

Kids Who Read

<http://kwr.co-nect.net/index.html>

Teachers can have their classes join a virtual book club to discuss literature, ask questions, share ideas, and reflect on a book.

Leaky Cauldron Web Site

<http://www.the-leaky-cauldron.org/>

Students can take part in book discussions concerning Harry Potter books.

Literary Book Club

<http://teach.fcps.net/lbc/>

Developed by Fayette County Public Schools, this site is designed to promote student literacy by encouraging students to read books and share their thoughts about those books. The site has posting forums and students can have interclass chats.

MysteryNet

<http://discuss.mysterynet.com/>

This site has several forums for discussions of authors, books, and characters.

Nancy Keane's Booktalks

<http://nancykeane.com/booktalks/>

Her site provides discussion blogs, books summaries, and links to excerpts of books for students.

On-Line Book Club for Kids

<http://students.ed.uiuc.edu/kmotsing/490NET/bookclub/BookClubHome.html>

This site is an online book discussion club for upper elementary and intermediate students; the books change every few months.

Parent Child Book Club Blog

<http://parentchild.blogspot.com/>

On this site parents and students post responses to weekly questions and research requirements as they have an online discussion about specific books.

Planet Book Club's Classroom Connection

<http://www.planetbookclub.com/>

This online discussion includes interactive components for both students and teachers through discussions of books.

Readers Club of America

<http://www.readersclubofamerica.com/>

This online book club offers readers a chance to experience sharing ideas and opinions with other readers nationwide on chosen books.

Readers Club

<http://www.readersclub.org/readinglog/>

This site provides an online reading log to record thoughts on books that are being read.

Scholastic's Flashlight Readers Club

<http://teacher.scholastic>

Here students can join with others, post comments, and play online activities.

The Secret Life of Bees

<http://Weblogs.hcrhs.k12.nj.us/beesbook/>

This online blog group creates a reader's study guide. Joiners have to make a minimum of two comments or posts that show thought and have clear connections to the book.

SeniorNet

<http://www.seniornet.org>

The Internet's oldest continuing books discussion site includes both fiction and nonfiction book discussions.

Spaghetti Book Club

<http://www.spaghettibookclub.com/>

This site provides a program to integrate reading, writing, art, and technology by teaching students how to write and illustrate book reviews, which are then published on the Spaghetti Book Club Web site.

Yahooligans! Book Club

<http://yahooligans.yahoo.com/content/bookclub/>

This site features celebrities sharing their favorite children's books and has children's recommendations and reviews of book club titles.

Tools for Creating Your Own Discussion Sites

Blog Sites

Blog hosting sites on the Web have become very popular. Some common online blog sites that can be joined for free include:

Blogger

<http://www.blogger.com/>

This service from Google provides Web tools for individuals to use to publish blogs to the Web (see Figure 5.10).

Bloglines

<http://www.bloglines.com/>

This service from Ask Jeeves provides Web tools for individuals to use to publish blogs to the Web.

BlogMeister by David Warlick

<http://landmark-project.com/blogmeister/>

On this site teachers can set up a password-protected class site for students to participate.

GreatestJournal

<http://www.greatestjournal.com/>

This site allows users to create an online journal or diary though the Internet.

LiveJournal

<http://www.livejournal.com/>

Also known as LJ, this site allows Internet users to keep an online journal or diary.

My Space

<http://www.myspace.com/>

My space is a blog hosting service that is available for free.

November Learning

<http://www.novemberlearning.com/Default.aspx?tabid=39>

This communication software for educators helps schools and organizations provide a safe and globally collaborative environment.

SchoolBlogs

<http://www.schoolblogs.com/>

Set up by a former teacher, the goal of this blog is to make available the potential of Weblogs to the educational world free of charge.

Xanga

<http://www.xanga.com/>

Xanga is a journal-hosting service, largely used by teenagers and young adults, but is open to anyone at least 13 years old.

Figure 5.10 Blogger is a service from Google that provides Web tools for individuals to use to publish blogs to the Web.

Blog Software

A more advanced blog project, rather than using a hosting service, is to have students generate their blogs on a local server or computer which has blog software. Using this software, a teacher or library media specialist and a school computer tech could install the software to allow students to publish their blogs on their own school Web site or a third-party site. While these installable blog programs may provide greater flexibility and power than subscription services, they require programming knowledge and expertise to set up the Web sites, as the programs are written in PHP and use a My SQL database. Some free common installable blog programs include:

Nucleus CMS <http://www.nucleuscms.org/>

b2evolution <http://b2evolution.net/>

bBlog <http://www.bblog.com/>

boastMachine <http://boastology.com/>

Serendipity <http://s9y.org/>

WordPress <http://wordpress.org/>

Figure 5.11   World Press is an example blog program that is available for download and installation.

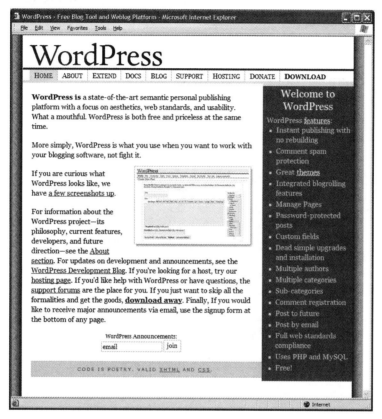

Wiki Farms

Wiki farms provide online servers that can be joined, often for free, where users can build their own wiki pages. The following are a few examples of wiki farms that can be joined for free.

JotSpot

<http://www.jot.com/>

JotSpot is a wiki farm service with a WYSIWGY (what you see is what you get) interface, allowing five user personal accounts for up to 20 pages free of charge.

pbwiki (peanut butter wiki)

<http://pbwiki.com/>

This site provides free, ad-free, password-protected wikis with easy set up. These wikis can be made public, but are not publicly editable.

Riters.com

<http://www.riters.com/>

Riters.com is a free wiki farm service.

Schtuff

<http://www.schtuff.com/>

This free wiki service has extra features like tagging, custom permissions, and an image gallery.

SeedWiki

<http://www.seedwiki.com/

This free wiki farm is supported by Google-ads placed at the bottom of the page.

Wikicities

<http://www.wikicities.com/wiki/Wikicities>

This wiki hosting site has a collection of wiki Web sites that are editable. Individuals can also start their own wiki in Wikicities.

wikihost.org

<http://wikihost.org/>

This site is a free wiki farm service.

Wikispaces

<http://www.wikispaces.org/>

Wikispaces is an online wiki server where individuals can easily build Web pages with other people.

Wiki Software

For a more advanced project, a teacher could install wiki software for students to use on a school network or computer. A number of wiki programs are available as open source software for free download. While these installable wiki programs can provide greater flexibility and power, they do require programming knowledge and technical expertise to set up.

FlexWiki <http://www.flexwiki.com/> (server)

MediaWiki <http://www.mediawiki.org/wiki/MediaWiki> (server)

Notebook Wiki <http://notebook.wjduquette.com/> (desktop: Linux, Mac and Windows)

Twiki <http://www.twiki.org/> (server)

wikidPad <ttp://www.jhorman.org/wikidPad/> (desktop: Windows)

WikiWikiWeb <http://c2.com/cgi/wiki?WikiWikiWeb> (server)

Wikka Wiki <http://wikka.jsnx.com/WikkaOnMacOSX> (server/desktop: Mac)

XWiki <http://www.xwiki.org/> (server)

References

Beach, Richard and Dana Lundell. *Early adolescents' use of computer-mediated communication in writing and reading.* In D. Reinking, M. C. McKenna, L. Labbo, and R. Kieffer (eds.), *Handbook of Literacy and Technology: Transformations in a Post-typographic World.* (Vol. 379: 93–112.) Mahwah, NJ: Lawrence Erlbaum Associates (1998).

Cavanaugh, Cathy. *Clips from the Classroom: Learning with Technology.* Upper Saddle River, NJ: Prentice Hall (2005).

Colgan, Craig. "What's in a Blog? Educators discover the newest form of intimate and immediate conversation." *American School Board Journal* (2005). Electronic version retrieved July 2005 from <http://www.asbj.com/2005/07/0705coverstory2.html>.

Kamil, Michael (2003). "Adolescents and Literacy: Reading for the 21st Century." *Alliance for Excellent Education* (2003). Retrieved April 2005 from <http://www.all4ed.org/publications/AdolescentsAndLiteracy.pdf>.

Keane, Nancy. "FAQ." *Nancy Keane's Booktalks – Quick and Simple* (2005). Retrieved July 2005 from <http://nancykeane.com/booktalks/>.

Lambright, Lesley L. "Creating a dialogue: Socratic seminars and educational reform." *Community College Journal.* 65 (1995): 30-34.

Lenhart, Amanda, John Horrigan, and Deborah Fallows. "Content Creation Online." *Pew Internet & American Life Project.* Released Sunday, February 29, 2004. Retrieved July 2005 from <http://www.pewInternet.org/pdfs/PIP_Content_Creation_Report.pdf>.

Walters, Johnny. "Virtual Circles: Using Technology to Enhance Literature Circles & Socratic Seminars." *Meridian* (2003). Retrieved April 2005 from <http://www.ncsu.edu/meridian/sum2003/circles/circles.pdf>.

Wilhelm, Jeff. "Literacy by Design: Why Is All This Technology So Important?" *Voices from the Middle,* Vol. 7, No. 3. (March 2000): 4.

Winer, Dave. "The History of Weblogs." *Weblogs.com News* (n.d.). Retrieved July 2005 from <http://newhome.Weblogs.com/historyOfWeblogs>.

The Literature Circle in Distance Learning

The American Association of School Librarians (AASL) Information Literacy Standards addressed in this chapter:

- Information Literacy: 1
- Independent Learning: 4 and 5
- Social Responsibility: 7, 8, and 9

The International Society for Technology in Education (ISTE) Technology Foundation Standards for All Students addressed in this chapter:

- Basic operations and concepts: 1.1 and 1.2
- Social, ethical, and human issues: 2.2 and 2.3
- Technology productivity tools: 3.1 and 3.2
- Technology communications tools: 4.1 and 4.2
- Technology research tools: 5.1, 5.2, and 5.3
- Technology problem-solving and decision-making tools: 6.2

For more information on these standards, see page ix.

This chapter examines how distance learning technologies can be integrated into a literature circle discussion. Distance learning takes place when students are removed from one another or from the instructor by either distance or time. A single student, a few students, a discussion group, or even a whole class—depending on the needs of the students and the availability of the technology—can apply distance learning to the literature circle. Integrating distance learning into the literature circle offers flexibility in the time, place, and pace of the discussion. A resource list with samples of distance learning course space environments is included at the end of this chapter.

Integration into Distance Learning

There are three basic designs for integrating the literature circle into the distance learning environment. The first takes place in a distance learning school where students only meet in a virtual environment. The next connects a portion of a class that needs to participate remotely, such as students who are homeschooled or are hospital or homebound and are unable to physically attend school. The third design involves members from different classes or entire classes participating with each other remotely. For example, similar classes in two schools can connect, or older students at a high school can join with younger students at a middle or elementary school.

In each of the above cases, using standard literature circle activities is inappropriate, if not impossible. Instead, because the interactions take place in a virtual environment, students' communication becomes more telecollaborative. Since students already use computer-based tools for communication, they can also use the technologies to support their literature circle roles. This moves the activities more to the right of the technology-enhanced continuum. An instructor might also find it easier to provide students the option to use a digital version of the text, which moves reading material more to the right, creating a fully technology-integrated approach (see Figure 6.1).

Figure 6.1 Continuum of using technology in the literature circle for distance learning.

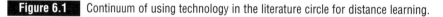

in person   COMMUNICATION   telecollaboration

none   TECHNOLOGY ACTIVITY   all

The availability of today's information resources and technology networking provides students with the option to have reading instruction delivered by computer through distance learning. Today any student with a computer and Internet access can take part in an educational program delivered to her through the Internet, from a single lesson, to a course, to a whole program.

Distance Learning in Schools Today

According to a National Center for Education Statistics report (NCES and Phipps 2002), a survey of over 3,500 higher education institutions found that 78% of four-year and 62% of two-year public colleges and universities used distance learning. The survey also found an increase at all higher education institutions in the number of courses using distance education, with an increase of 11% over a two-year period, from 33% to 44% (NCES 2002). An estimated 1.6 million college students across the nation took at least one course through distance learning in 1999 (U.S. DOE 2000). This trend is reflected in the K-12 educational setting. The U.S. Department of Education's National Center for Education Statistics (NCES) found that one-third (36%) of public school districts and 9% of public schools had students enrolled in distance education courses in 2002-2003 (NCES 2005, CNN.com 2005). Susan Patrick, then director of the U.S. Department of Education's Office of Educational Technology, stated that in 2004 between 40,000 and 50,000 students from 37 states attended a virtual school on the Internet (Fording 2004). The Department of Education goes so far as to predict that within the next ten years every state and most schools will offer a form of virtual school instruction to their students (U.S. DOE 2004). At least fifteen states currently offer virtual schooling to supplement regular classes or provide for special needs. One example is the Florida Virtual School (FLVS), a nationally accredited state public high school that delivers Internet-based instruction to grades 8 through 12. Started in 1997, FLVS currently offers over 80 courses to a growing student population that is now surpassing 33,000 (See Figure 6.2). The current faculty of the school includes over 200 certified teachers residing throughout the state (FLVS 2005). These trends demonstrate that distance learning will be a common component of education tomorrow and, for many educators and students, it is part of education today.

Figure 6.2   Florida Virtual School Enrollment Numbers 1996-2005.

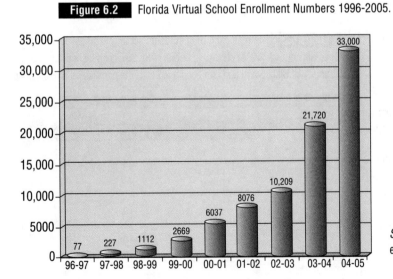

Source: FLVS statistics of enrollment/participation.

A **course management system** is a computer program that facilitates and organizes learning by helping teachers and learners with course administration and providing delivery of instructional materials. Course management systems are also known as Learning Management Systems (LMS), Virtual Learning Environments (VLE), Computer-Mediated Communication (CMC) in education, and Online Education. A course management system usually includes templates for creating information and content pages, discussion forums, chat, and assessment tools. Teachers fill in the templates and then release them for learners to use.

Synchronous learning is a learning event in which the interactions happen simultaneously in real-time. It requires that learners attend class at a scheduled time and participate "live" or be present in the same space or time. This type of learning can occur in a classroom, or via technology. Synchronous communication examples include chats and instant messages, because all participants must be at their computers, online, and using communication at the same time. Live audio or video of an instructor streaming out to students on the Internet is an example of a synchronous teaching event.

Asynchronous learning is a learning event that takes place when the interaction is delayed over time, and members do not have to interact at the same time. Students participating by e-mail or a discussion forum are examples of asynchronous communication. One person can send a note to another person and the recipient need not be online to receive the e-mail. An instructor putting up Web pages or setting up discussion questions is an example of an asynchronous teaching event.

To Sync or Async

Most of today's K-12 distance education involves students who take only one or two courses, usually in high school, but some distance learning programs do extend to middle school and even to elementary school. Students usually participate in the distance learning environment using a course management system or tool (see Figure 6.3) such as Blackboard (<www.blackboard.com>) and WebCT (<www.Webct.com/>). Students use the distance learning environment either synchronously—in real time—or asynchronously. For example, an educator who wants to set up a literature circle discussion between two classrooms, in two different schools, for students to all go online at the same time, can set up a synchronous discussion. Students interact using tools such as whiteboards, chat rooms, instant messaging, and videoconferencing. Some states have projects like the Two Way Interactive Connections in Education (TWICE) of Michigan, which assists in organizing videoconferencing in K-12 education (<http://www.twice.cc/read>). An Internet or videoconference based system benefits a literature circle situation in which one or two students are unable to physically attend class, because they can still participate virtually. If the instructor developed a long-term project, or if students could not get online at the same time, then the discussion circle could be held asynchronously. In this case, students would use tools such as threaded discussions and file posting to collaborate.

Figure 6.3 Screen capture of students posting to an asynchronous booktalk about available electronic books in Blackboard's discussion board. Property of Blackboard and has been used with the permission of Blackboard.

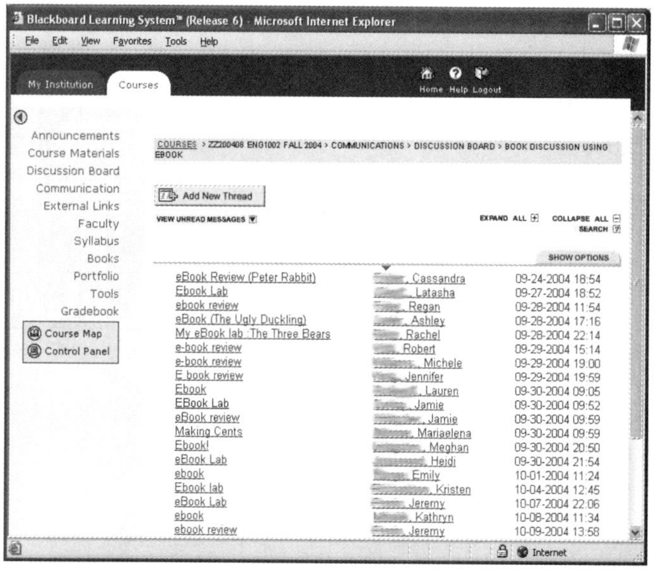

Other Populations

Students who may prefer or need distance learning in order to participate with other students in a literature circle include homeschooled, hospitalized, and homebound students. These students are usually unable to go to a school. In the distance learning environment, a group of homeschooled students, who can be widely separated by geography, can set up and use a literature circle to discuss their reading. A teacher or library media specialist can set up a virtual literature circle using course management software and then give students access to the system. In this way, a student out of school for an extended period of time because of an illness or disability can still work with his or her class through the virtual environment.

The Web-based learning environment can itself be an accommodation for special needs students. As most Web-based courses are asynchronous, they provide accommodations required by many students with special needs. Assistive technology specialists from the Florida Assistive Technology Education Network (ATEN) stated that to accommodate students with special needs, instructors should expect students to communicate. They should provide students with opportunities to interact with others, with varied models of print use; provide choices—and wait for them to respond; and provide opportunities to communicate (2002). All of these accommodations are inherent in most asynchronous distance learning environments and can be applied to the literature circle.

> **Homeschooling** means the education of school-aged children is under their parents' general monitoring, replacing full-time attendance at a campus school. Homeschooled students may enroll part time at a school or group together to share instruction with other families, but most of their educational program is under the direct oversight of parents. Homeschooling has been on the increase for decades. During the 1990-91 school year there were between 250,000 and 350,000 students homeschooled nationwide; this number increased to over a million (1,096,000) by the year 2003 (NCES 2003, Lines 1998).
>
> **Hospital or homebound** students are unable to attend school for extended periods of time, usually for medical reasons. According to U.S. government statistics, approximately 0.5% (26,000 in 1999) of the student population is classified as hospital or homebound under the IDEA law (U.S. DOE 2002a).

The Distance Learning Literature Circle

Using today's technologies to enhance literature circle assignments allows readers options to not only interact in person, but also through telecommunication applications including course spaces, e-mail, Web blogs, chatrooms, and digital whiteboards. The president of a virtual high school states that the well-designed online course can use communication and collaboration tools to foster high levels of student-student and student-teacher interactions and that online courses should have a variety of assessment activities to meet students' individual learning styles and needs (Pape 2005).

The integration of distance learning technologies into literature circle activities provides opportunities for students to interact along a continuum, from fully face-to-face to fully online, from one outside student participating to a full class of students. In some learning circle activities, students interact with each other in an online environment, such as Scholastic's Connect & Collaborate site (see Figure 6.4).

A set of technology-enhanced literature circle activities for distance learning is provided at the end of this chapter.

Figure 6.4 Scholastic's Classport online environment can be used to create an online literature circle.

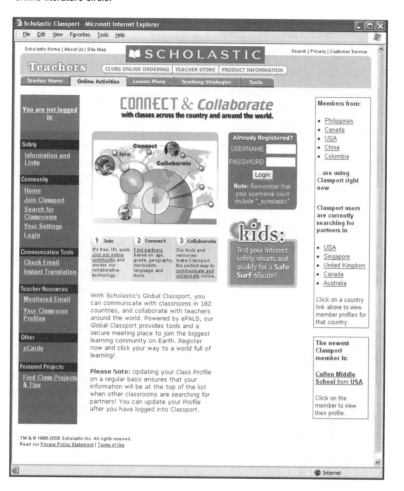

Effective Distance Learning

Cathy Cavanaugh (2004) in her book, *Development and Management of Virtual Schools: Issues and Trends,* identifies 44 success factors that can make distance learning effective. These success factors for effective distance learning instruction are divided into three areas: Resources for Instruction, Results and Achievement, and Instructional Practices. In an effective distance-learning environment, the instructional focus shifts to a more student centered paradigm. The instructional practices aim at developing independent learners. Effective communication and community building are essential foundations for all events. All of these practices fit well into the literature circle model. While students work together online as a group to communicate and collaborate about the book topic, they are independent workers within their reader roles. The literature circle is a student-centered activity, which is also a cooperative learning activity.

Dr. C. Cavanaugh's Success Factors for the Practices of Online Instruction (Cavanaugh 2004):

- Focus on content and students
- Relevant and important skills and knowledge addressed in courses
- Structured information presented in motivating context
- Social strategies to promote student comfort, control, challenge
- Fast feedback from instructors to students
- Consistent and accessible design throughout each course
- Highly interactive activities for student engagement
- Authentic communication among students, instructors and experts
- Course activities designed to maximize student motivation
- Activities focused on high-level cognitive skills
- Development of information literacy
- Development of applied technical skills

Sample Distance Learning Literature Circles

Figure 6.5 Screen capture of TWICE's Read Across America project (<http://www.twice.cc/read>).

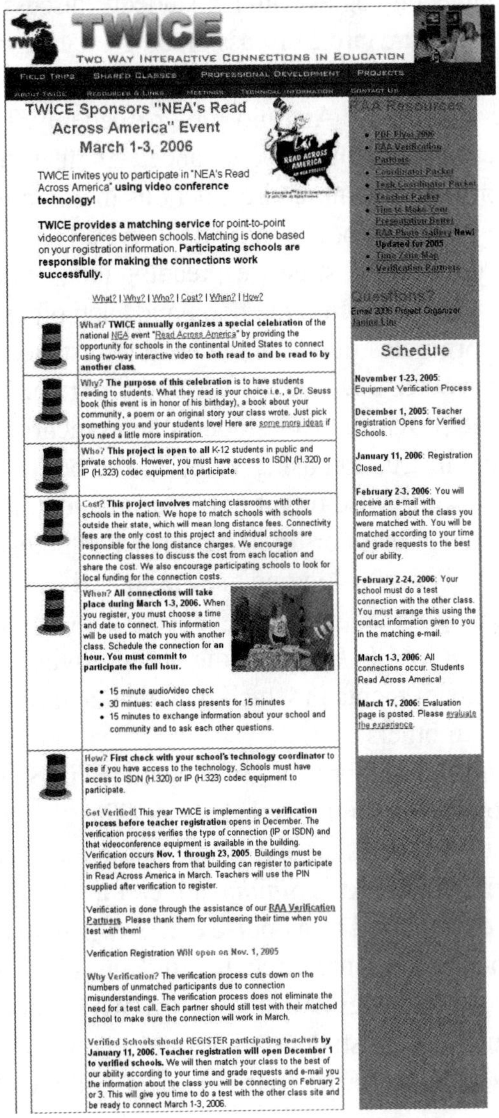

Several school systems have begun integrating literature circles with distance learning. These situations have enabled students to interact beyond the school boundaries, by including students among different schools, different districts, and even different cities. Some schools facilitate distance literature circles using videoconferencing technologies while others use an Internet-based system.

Videoconferencing Literature Circles

One video-based distance-learning program that used a literature circle format was the Sharing Perspectives project in Indiana, IL (DIAL 2000). In this project students worked in virtual groups reading critically and sharing their thoughts about books. The project linked students in different cities, connecting suburban fifth and sixth grade classes with urban fifth grade classes along with Indiana University (IU) students. Student groups with IU students serving as facilitators discussed through videoconferencing *Flying Solo* by Richard Fletcher.

Another videoconferencing example linked students and teachers from different school districts in a project developed by the New York State Distance Learning Consortium (NYSDLC n.d.). The "Literature Live!" program balanced groups of students from two different school districts who met and interacted in the videoconferencing environment to hold booktalks and literature circle discussions.

The Two Way Interactive Connections in Education (TWICE) is a national project developed in Michigan which organizes videoconferencing between K-12 schools to enable the schools to participate in the National Education Association's "Read Across America" project (see Figure 6.5). TWICE provides a matching service for point-to-point videoconferences to be set up between schools. The TWICE project is open to all K-12 public and private schools. Participating schools connect for an hour either using ISDN or IP equipment at a specific time when students use the two-way interactive video to both read to and be read to by another class.

Online Internet Literature Circles

An Internet-based literature circle project that uses blogs for discussions was developed by Shari Bithell, a sixth-grade teacher in California (PD-ROM 2005). Ms. Bithell incorporates distance-learning technologies with her students' discussion groups as they participate in online literature circle discussion blogs, partnering each literature circle group with preservice teachers.

In another California project at the San Antonio Junior Academy, The Online Literature Circle is a Web-enhanced course for advanced English students (AVLN 2005). Here students perform the literature circle actions in an online environment with other students, researching books to read, cooperatively deciding on books, learning specific critical questioning strategies, reading independently, and then using high level thinking skills to discuss the book and each other's work.

A regional program that incorporates literature circles into distance learning is the English 112 class in New Brunswick's Distance Learning program. This course for high school students in the province gives students an asynchronous course for online, anywhere, anytime instruction using WebCT. The online format allows students access to courses that otherwise might not be available to them, usually because of scheduling conflicts, illness or limited course availability in their own schools. The English 112 course is a year-long course composed of six learning modules. Some of the learning modules in the English class consist of an interactive *Literature Circle* and a *Writing Workshop*. In the online environment, students complete ongoing reading assignments in which they read and respond to books of their choice and interact with others.

The *Netlibris* project (http://www.netlibris.net) in Finland (SITES: M2 2001) is an example of a national online literature circle project. This project is divided into three subsections: First is *Matilda*, an online literature circle for students 7 to 12 years old (see Figure 6.6); next is *Sinuhe,* a literature circle open to all students 12 to 15 years old and can be used as a course elective or with a course; and finally *Odysseia,* which is an online literature circle for students 15 to 20 years old. In 2000, the Matilda project alone had over 250 students from 11 schools participating. In their online literature circles, students choose together and read the "book of the month," they keep personal reader response journals, and they have discussions about books in a Web-based discussion board or by exchanging e-mail within their groups. At a school, the *Netlibris* literature circle groups usually meet weekly while the online book discussions continue daily, with most students participating on average two to three times a week.

Figure 6.6 Sample student discussion from the Matilda project on Hans Christian Anderson's *The Ugly Duckling* (<http://www.netlibris.net/international/>).

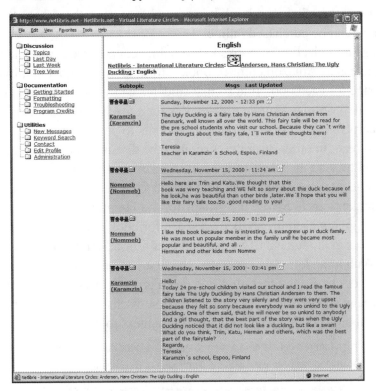

Educator Collaboration

Teachers and library media specialists can collaborate when working with literature circles that take place either partially or fully through virtual mediums. Library media specialists have an essential role in coordinating and assisting with activities such as videoconferencing. Educators and library media specialists should work together with students to identify high-interest reading topics and texts. The library media specialist can assist teachers and students by assembling book collections, coordinating interlibrary loan, and creating accessible versions of text. She can work with individual teachers to identify digitally available forms of texts to use in their class either as the books for the circle discussion or as associated research and resource materials. Library media specialists can join the virtual class, becoming additional instructors, providing instruction to students concerning online activities and behaviors along with instruction concerning research strategies and online resources.

The local library media specialist can work with library media specialists who are at schools where the participating virtual students attend physically. They can coordinate with students for book and computer access within the library media center, creating comfortable areas within the centers where students can go to participate with their virtual classes. School-based Web pages can also assist students in "getting" to class and with instruction or links to additional resource materials.

Classroom Management

For a distance learning literature circle to flow smoothly, teachers should establish procedures for both managing the technology resources and student access to those technologies.

First, assemble a list of books about an academic topic or theme that your students could use as a reading activity for learning. For a distance learning situation, if students are not physically in a school, it is advisable to use either books that are available online or can be purchased online.

Next, post the selection of books in the online course space. One strategy is to use resources such as Amazon.com for book information. Create a link to the Amazon Web page for each book title so that students can view the page to read the covers and book descriptions. Another strategy is for a teacher to post his booktalks and reading excerpts in the course space. Ask students to post a listing of the books that they want to read, in order of preference, into the discussion board of the online class, or ask them to send their lists to the course instructor by e-mail.

Divide students into groups based on their book selections; construct groups of four to five students each. Set up the groups for the literature circle in the online discussion board, giving each group its own space for book discussions.

Assign roles to the students. One method uses a Java Script random assignment/ role generator. With a random role generator, the first person to make a note in the discussion forum or chat is assigned that role (see Figure 6.7). As an alternative, the instructor can assign students to roles during the first discussion round. With each round of the discussion, students will advance to the next role on the list.

Figure 6.7   Using a random role generator to assign student roles in a virtual literature circle. Property of Blackboard and has been used with the permission of Blackboard.

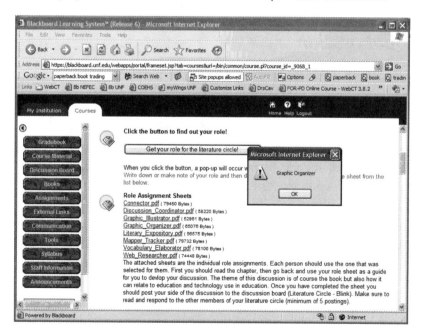

Now students should have the opportunity to independently read the assigned reading material (pages, chapter, section), making notes in a reading journal and working on their roles. In one of my own classes, the book chapters that I assigned to students were already online, so I made links to the book chapters within the online course. Students had the option to either read the material on their computer as an eBook or to print it out and read a paper copy instead.

Make sure for each discussion round that someone in the group is the Discussion Coordinator. This person also becomes the discussion moderator. She is in charge of the discussion and will act as a liaison between the group and the instructor.

Discussions may be either synchronous or asynchronous, depending on the class situation, learning goals, and the availability of the technology.

Synchronous Discussion

(Uses electronic classroom tools such as chat, whiteboards, instant messaging.)
Group members all go online at the same time to discuss the reading. The discussion occurs using synchronous tools such as the chat room. For example, in Blackboard an area in the Collaboration tools is called the Virtual Classroom (see Figure 6.8) which includes chat and whiteboard tools. As members post information according to their roles, other members respond. You may wish to have a minimum specified number of responses required to help get the discussion moving. I inform my students that it is acceptable to give responses like "I agree" or "that's right," but those responses do not count toward their requirements. They must make their statements and then support them.

Figure 6.8 Blackboard's Collaboration tool Virtual Classroom has live chat and an interactive whiteboard sections. Property of Blackboard and has been used with the permission of Blackboard.

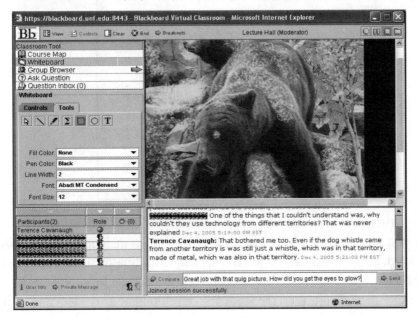

Asynchronous Discussion

(Uses electronic classroom tools such as e-mail, forums, discussion boards, and posting attachments.)
In this case the discussion may take place over a day or a few days, as members post their work, read what others have written, and post responses. Each member of the group is asked to post what they did in relation to their role sheet. All group members are expected to read each of the other group member's postings. I also have a requirement that they should respond to a minimum of three postings with

the same response criteria as above in the synchronous discussion. The Discussion Coordinator helps move the discussion along, making sure that each member posts the required information, making sure that each posting is read by other members, and asking his own questions to the group.

Figure 6.9 Literature circle discussion taking place in Blackboard's Discussion Board. Property of Blackboard and has been used with the permission of Blackboard.

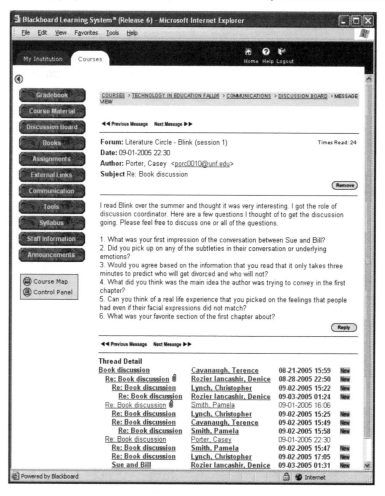

Instructors should monitor the progress of online discussions and join a discussion at any time by asking questions or giving an insight. Once the discussion is completed, either the instructor or Discussion Coordinator should print out or save a copy of the discussion for assessment and archive. These printouts can be an excellent tool for evaluation of the students' development as readers and writers.

Course Management Systems/Tools

The following are a few of the available tools that educators and school districts can use to facilitate distance learning instruction.

Subscription (fee based):

WebCT <http://www.Webct.com/>
Blackboard <http://www.blackboard.com/>
eBoard <http://www.eboard.com>

Open Source (free):

Moodle <http://moodle.org/>
Sakai Project <http://www.sakaiproject.org/>
Manhattan Virtual Classroom <http://manhattan.sourceforge.net/>
Wordcircle CMS <http://wordcircle.org/>
Claroline <http://www.claroline.net/>
Fle3 Learning Environment <http://fle3.uiah.fi/>
Classport <http://www.scholastic.com/classport/>

Conclusion

If, as educators, we believe in "no child left behind," then we must ensure that sufficient services, approaches, and educational options exist for instruction of all students. Discussion circles can be easily and effectively served using a range of distance learning strategies. Online learning will become more common in the future, and it is important to allow students to interact using today's telecommunication tools and skills.

References

ATEN (Assistive Technology Education Network of Florida). (2000). Assistive Technology: Unlocking Human Potential through Technology. Presentation at the University of South Florida.

AVLN (Adventist Virtual Learning Network). "2005 AVLN Online Conference: Presentations – The Online Literature Circle." *Adventist Virtual Learning Network* (2005). Retrieved August 2005 from <http://www.avln.org/conference/2005/presentations.htm>.

Cavanaugh, Cathy. "Distance Learning Success Factors in the Resources-Processes-Results Cycle and Virtual School Accreditation" in *Development and Management of Virtual Schools: Issues and Trends,* Cavanaugh, C. editor. Hershey, PA: Idea Group Publishing (2004).

Cavanaugh, Cathy and Terence Cavanaugh. "Distance Learning Success Factors in the Resources-Processes-Results Cycle and the Web Accessibility Guidelines." Paper presented at the 2004 Sloan-C International Conference on Online Learning. Orlando, FL (2004). Retrieved August 2005 from <http://www.unf.edu/~tcavanau/presentations/SLOAN/paperRPRaccess.htm>.

CNN.com Distance learning becoming part of school life. CNN (March 3, 2005). Article available online. Retrieved April 2005 from <http://www.cnn.com/2005/EDUCATION/03/03/distance.education.ap>.

DIAL (Distance InterActive Learning) Sharing Perspectives. *Distance InterActive Learning* (2000). Retrieved July 2005 from <http://crlt.indiana.edu/dial/p_sharingperspec.html >.

FLVS (Florida Virtual School). "About Us." *Florida Virtual School* (2005). Retrieved July 2005 from <http://www.flvs.net>.

Fording, Laura. "Virtual classrooms are still outnumbered by brick-and-mortar schools, but they are gaining popularity. A glimpse of the future." *Newsweek* (March 30, 2004). Retrieved July 2005 from <http://msnbc.msn.com/id/4633126/>.

Lines, Patricia M. "Homeschoolers: Estimating Numbers and Growth." National Institute on Student Achievement, Curriculum, and Assessment, Office of Educational Research and Improvement, *U.S. Department of Education* (1998). Retrieved August 2005 from <http://www.ed.gov/offices/OERI/SAI/homeschool/>.

NCES (National Center for Educational Statistics). "1.1 Million Homeschooled Students in the United States in 2003." *National Center for Educational Statistics* (2003). Retrieved August 2005 from <http://nces.ed.gov/nhes/homeschool/>.

NCES (National Center for Educational Statistics). "Distance Education Courses for Public Elementary and Secondary School Students: 2002-2003." *National Center for Educational Statistics* (2005). Retrieved August 2005 from <http://nces.ed.gov/pubsearch/pubsinfo.asp?pubid=2005010>.

NCES (National Center for Educational Statistics) and Phipps, R. A. "Access To Postsecondary Education: What is the Role of Technology?" Report Written for the National Postsecondary Education Cooperative (NPEC). *National Center for Educational Statistics* (2002). Retrieved April 2004 from <http://nces.ed.gov/npec/papers/PDF/WhatRoleTechnology.pdf>.

New Brunswick DOE (Department of Education). "e-Learning – Distance Learning." New Brunswick Department of Education (2005). Retrieved August 2005 from <http://www.gnb.ca/0000/as/dl-e.asp>.

NYSDLC (New York State Distance Learning Consortium). "NYSDLC Discussion Paper." New York State Distance Learning Consortium (n.d.). Retrieved July 2005 from <http://www.nysdlc.org/WhitePaper.shtm>.

Pape, Liz. "High School on the Web: What you need to now about offering online courses." *American School Board Journal.* July 2005: Vol. 192, No. 7. Retrieved July 2005 from <http://www.asbj.com/2005/07/0705coverstory.html>.

PD-ROM (Professional Development Resources Online for Mathematics). "PD-ROM Staff." *Professional Development Resources Online for Mathematics* (2005). Retrieved August 2005 from <http://pdrom.coursepath.org/info/staff.cfm>.

SITES: M2 (The Second Information Technology in Education Study: Module 2). "Narrative Case Report – NETLIBRIS LITERATURE CIRCLES." International Association for the Evaluation of Educational Achievement (2001). Retrieved June 2005 from <http://sitesm2.org/sitesm2_search/docs/FI005_narrative.pdf>.

TWICE (Two Way Interactive Connections in Education). "TWICE Sponsors 'NEA's Read Across America' Event March 1-3, 2006." Two Way Interactive Connections in Education (2005). Retrieved July 2005 from <http://www.twice.cc/read>.

U.S. DOE (Department of Education). "Getting Ready Pays Off: A Report for National College Week." U.S. Department of Education. Washington, DC (2000). Retrieved April 2004 from <http://www.ed.gov/offices/OPE/News/collegeweek/collegeweekpdf.pdf>.

U.S. DOE (Department of Education). "Toward A New Golden Age In American Education: How the Internet, the law and today's students are revolutionizing expectations." U.S. Department of Education. Washington, DC (2004).

Discussion Coordinator^(tech-DL)

Name: _____ Group: _____

Book: _____

Author: _____

Reading Assignment: page _____ to page_____

Assignment:

Your job is to develop a list of questions that your group might want to discuss about this book or part of book. Your task is to act as the discussion moderator and help people talk over the big ideas in the reading and share the other members' reactions through a discussion board, Weblog, e-mail or chat. Usually the best questions come from your own thoughts, feelings, and concerns that occur as you read. You can list these ideas below during or after your reading and then post them online for your group to discuss. If you want, you may use some of the example questions below to help you develop the topics for your group. Part of your job is also to make sure that each group member contributes to the discussion session.

Possible discussion questions or topics for today:

1. _____

2. _____

3. _____

4. _____

5. _____

Sample Questions:

- What went through your mind while you read this book or passage?
- How did you feel while reading this part of the book?
- How would someone summarize this section?
- What was the main point discussed in this book or section?
- At what point did today's reading remind you of any real-life experiences?
- What questions did you have when you finished this section?
- Did anything in this book or section surprise you?
- Describe one or two of the most important ideas presented in the text.
- Predict some things you think will be talked about next.

Vocabulary Elaborator*(tech-DL)*

Name: _____ Group: _____

Book: _____

Author: _____

Reading Assignment: page _____ to page_____

Assignment:

Your job is to develop a list of words for your group to define in the context of this book or part of book. Your task is to help define these words from the reading and share with the other members through a discussion board, Weblog, e-mail or chat. The words you select to define should be words that you or other members of your group cannot pronounce, define, or understand in the way they are presented. To find your words:

1. First, point to the unexplained word and then underline or highlight it.

2. Next, read the sentence containing the unexplained word.

   a. If you cannot comprehend the meaning of the word, read the preceding sentence to try to figure out the definition.

   b. If you still don't have a definition for the marked word, then read the next sentence after the marked word.

3. Lastly, use a dictionary to check the definition of the word. Use either an interactive dictionary that occurs when you highlight the word or visit an online dictionary site such as:

   ■ **The Internet Picture Dictionary** <http://www.pdictionary.com/>

   ■ **The Online Rhyming Dictionary** <http://www.writeexpress.com/online2.html>

   ■ **Different types of dictionaries** <http://directory.google.com/Top/Kids_and_Teens/ School_Time/Reference_Tools/Dictionaries/>

   ■ **Online Slang Dictionary** <http://www.ocf.berkeley.edu/~wrader/slang/index.html>

   ■ **American Heritage Dictionary (online) – Bartleby** <http://www.bartleby.com/>

Usually dictionaries will have several meanings for a word, and it is important to look at each numbered definition and decide which one coincides with the marked word.

Words I have never heard before:

Words whose meaning I don't know:

Words I have seen before, but never used this way:

	Word	Page/Paragraph/Line	Definition
1			
2			
3			
4			
5			

Literary Expositor$^{(tech\text{-}DL)}$

Name: _____ Group: _____

Book: _____

Author: _____

Reading Assignment: page _____ to page_____

Assignment:

Your job is to select from the book or passage, by yourself or with help, several favorite or interesting passages. Your task is to select three or four of your favorite parts of the story to share aloud with your group members. As you read and find sections that you like, highlight the paragraphs and record the corresponding page numbers you enjoyed reading and want to hear read aloud. Possible reasons for selection include important, well written, humorous, informative, surprising, controversial, funny, confusing, and thought provoking.

     Once you have selected your sentences, use a microphone and software (such as Windows Sound Recorder) to record your sentences and upload them to the discussion site for the other members to download and play on their computers. After the book or section has been read in its entirety by the group, the Literary Expositor will record and upload his or her selected read-aloud sentences or paragraphs and identify for group members the location of his or her selections. During the playing of the read-aloud segment, the other group members will play and listen intently to your recordings as they read along with the sections, determine and then share, using a chat or the discussion board, what particular aspect of the reading they enjoyed the most. You must find at least three, but no more than five, sentences to read aloud to your group.

Page/Paragraph/Line	Reason	Sentence
1		
2		
3		
4		
5		

Graphic Illustrator(tech-DL)

Name: _____   Group: _____

Book: _____

Author: _____

Reading Assignment: page _____ to page_____

Assignment:

Your job is to draw two pictures into the whiteboard section that depicts the main idea and feeling in the narrative. Your task is to create illustrations in the online discussion section that show a character's interaction with other characters or story elements. After using the drawing tools to create your picture, add text labels to the parts to assist everyone with understanding your drawings. Also, draw pictures that show story or text ideas and then discuss your idea pictures with your group. You can use the shared whiteboard, or use the paint program then copy and paste the pictures to the whiteboard space. Once your pictures are finished, create a text box and write out a description of the characters' interaction in complete sentences and standard paragraph form. Use the space below to develop your paragraph drafts.

Draft Paragraph Descriptions: _____

_____

_____

_____

_____

_____

_____

_____

_____

_____

_____

_____

_____

_____

Graphic Organizer^(tech-DL)

Name: _____ Group: _____

Book: _____

Author: _____

Reading Assignment: page _____ to page_____

Assignment:

Your job is to create a content or concept map from the reading that helps your group gain a better understanding of the reading. Create your concept map from the reading with the main idea at the center or top and the related ideas moving out with descriptors connecting verbs. You can use the shared whiteboard space or create it with mind mapping software, such as Inspiration, and then copy and paste it to the whiteboard. You can also use other digital concept mapping tools and resources (many tools are available online) to create maps such as a Venn diagram, timeline, or concept web. Paste your concept map into the whiteboard space to share with the other group members and see if they have any other points or connections to add. You can make any type of graphic organizer you wish, or choose from the list below.

- **International Reading Association's Read•Write•Think**
  <http://www.readwritethink.org/student_mat/index.asp>
- **Education World Templates (doc)**
  <http://www.educationworld.com/tools_templates/>

Character Map | Timeline | Character Interaction | Story Line/Plot | Compare & Contrast (Venn)

Background Researcher^(tech-DL)

Name: _____ Group: _____

Book: _____

Author: _____

Reading Assignment: page _____ to page_____

Assignment:

Your job is to read from the text and identify when and where the writing occurred. Your task is to identify the historical time frame or location and research a topic related to that time or location of your choice. In the text, characters behave in a certain manner or events are described in a certain way that reflects a specific period in time or location. This is known as the setting. You should investigate a topic of interest that happened in that specific time period or location of the setting. If the book is not story based, then identify a fact from the reading and research that fact to find something of interest to you. From the reading, identify at least three statements that indicate the historical or locational (or factual) setting and write them in the space below. Then go online and find an associated Web site that you find interesting concerning that time or location. Share your findings and Web sites with your group members in the shared chat or discussion space, describing the site and how it relates to the reading, explaining why you found it interesting and sharing the site's URL.

Setting Statements:

Page/Paragraph/Line	Year/Location	Sentence
1		
2		
3		

Interesting Web sites findings:
URL – Title – Reading Associating – Description – Interest

_____

_____

_____

_____

_____

_____

Media Hunter *(tech-DL)*

Name: _____ Group: _____

Book: _____

Author: _____

Reading Assignment: page _____ to page_____

Assignment:

Your job is to read and identify from the text interesting aspects included in the text and then locate associated media to share with the other literacy circle group members. Your task is to identify some aspect from the reading and then search and find either images, sound files, or video related to that topic, time, or location. You can search to find media on a topic of interest that happened in that specific time period or location of the setting. If the book is not story based, then identify a fact from the reading and search for associated media concerning that fact. From the reading, identify at least three statements that indicate the historical or locational (or factual) setting and write them in the space below. Then go online and use media search tools and find associated images, sound files, or videos from Web sites. You can use the media search tools listed below or others you may know. These media files should be ones that you find interesting concerning that fact, time, or location. Share your findings and their Web sites' URLs by either copying and pasting the images onto the whiteboard or uploading the image, sound or video files to the shared discussion space for the other members to download and "play" on their computers and then comment on. Make sure you include the source URL in the shared chat or discussion space with your group members and state how the media relates to the reading.

Search Tools

- **Google Image Search** <http://images.google.com/>
- **Lycos Multimedia Search** <http://multimedia.lycos.com/>
- **Search Engine Watch listing of media search engines**
  <http://searchenginewatch.com/links/article.php/2156251>
- **National Archives media tools**
  <http://www.archives.gov/research_room/research_paths.html>

Page/Paragraph/Line	Year/Location	Sentence
1		
2		
3		

Media Web Sites Findings: URL – Format – Description – Relation

_____

_____

Web Researcher *(tech-DL)*

Name: _____ Group: _____

Book: _____

Author: _____

Reading Assignment: page _____ to page_____

Assignment:

Your job concerns the book, author, and content, where you create a summary book study or author study concerning the material you read, and construct a question you would like answered by the author (or another expert). If you decide to do a book study, then you would be looking at reviews or resources related to the book or its contents. Search for the book title and then review your results. If you have decided to do an author study, you will be looking for biographical data and information about the author such as who he is, what else has he written, when did he start writing, what else is he working on now, where is he from, when was he born. One way to start getting information on the book or author is to go to Amazon.com and search for the book. There you will find the start of some reviews and a link to the author's name. If you click on the name link, it should also produce a list of other books by that author currently for sale from Amazon. Don't think that one site is all you will need to visit. Find out if the author has a site. Look for a publisher site that may give you insight and information about the book or author. Find your sites and information, then copy and paste relevant portions into a word processor (don't forget to get the reference and URL), then combine your findings into a new summary. Post or share, using the online discussion space, your summary book or author study with your group. With your group, develop a question that you would like to ask the author of the book about the material. If your author or topic (expert) is not available from the list below, use a search engine with *ask author* and the author's name, or *ask expert* and the topic name as the keyword search terms. Many times authors are available to ask questions through e-mail. Consider asking an author or other expert your question (with teacher permission). When you get an answer, be sure to share it with your group and class.

- **Ask an Author** <http://www.ipl.org/div/kidspace/askauthor/AuthorLinks.html>
- **Ask an Expert** <http://cln.org/int_expert.html>
- **Ask Dr. Science** <http://www.drscience.com>
- **Ask Dr. Universe** <http://www.wsu.edu/DrUniverse/Contents.html>
- **Children's Literature Web Guide** <http://www.ucalgary.ca/~dkbrown/>
- **CLN Ask an Expert** <http://www.cln.org/int_expert.html>
- **ExpertCentral** <http://www.expertcentral.com>
- **Internet Public Library's Literary Criticism** <http://www.ipl.org/div/litcrit/>
- **Scientific American – Ask the Experts** <http://www.sciam.com/askexpert_directory.cfm>

My Question: _____

_____

_____

Connector^(tech-DL)

Name: _____ Group: _____

Book: _____

Author: _____

Reading Assignment: page _____ to page_____

Assignment:

Your job is to make connections from the reading to other experiences: to other texts, to yourself, or to any other things you have heard about or seen. Your task is to make statements that explain connections between what you are reading to something you have read in the past, some of your own personal experiences, or anything else in the world (for example, the news, movies, television programs, people). As you read, consider what you are reading and try to make the connections. You can create your own connections or use the examples below. In the shared discussion or chat space: state the page or location of the sentence you are connecting; copy and paste, rewrite or summarize the sentence; and then explain about the connection you are making.

Connection starters:

- This book reminds me of _____ (another text) because...
- I remember reading another book, _____, that also talked about ...
- This part of the reading reminds me of ...
- I felt like _____ (story character) when I ...
- If this had happened to me, I would have ...
- Something similar happened to me when ...
- The reading relates to my life by ...
- This reading reminds me of a news report I saw on television about ...
- This book reminds me of _____ (a movie) that was about ...

Connections:

Page	Sentence	Connection
1		
2		
3		

Mapper/Tracker *(tech-DL)*

Name: _____ Group: _____

Book: _____

Author: _____

Reading Assignment: page _____ to page_____

Assignment:

Your job concerns the book's characters or content and the location. You will create some form of map representation of the reading content. The map can be a tracking map, a comparison map, or collage or series of location maps. The question you are trying to answer is where is the content from the reading occurring? A **tracking map** is one that provides a visual display that follows or shows in order where events took place. A **comparison map** is one that shows your actual location relative to the material in the reading. The **map collage** contains a collection of various maps of locations presented in the reading. In each case, you should edit the maps, such as adding marks onto the map image to specify location. Start by finding location information from the reading, noting where it occurs in the text and the locations that the text is describing. Now make your map. One way this can be done is to copy the map into a drawing or paint program, use the tools to add marks, or waypoints, trackways, and character or event names onto the map to identify the reading location or locations. Once you have completed your map or maps, write a descriptive paragraph that explains your map materials. Now share your map material with your group by either copying and pasting the images onto the whiteboard or uploading the images and the description to the shared discussion space for the other members to view on their computers and then comment on.

What type of map are you creating? ☐ Tracking ☐ Comparison ☐ Collage

- **CIA World Factbook** <http://www.cia.gov/cia/publications/factbook/index.html>
- **Yahoo Maps** <http://maps.yahoo.com/>
- **Google Maps** <http://maps.google.com/>
- **Mapquest** <http://www.mapquest.com/>
- **Microsoft TerraServer** <http://terraserver.microsoft.com/>

Location notes

Page/Paragraph/Line	Location Statement
1	
2	
3	

Map Description: _____

_____

Appendix

Sample Rubrics and
Scoring Guides

Table A.1

Literature Circle: Self-Evaluation

Name: _____ Circle/Group: _____

Book: _____

☐ I brought my book to class.

☐ I read the section that I was supposed to before each discussion.

☐ I participated by sharing about the book with my circle or group.

☐ I actively listened to other members of my circle or group about the book.

☐ I worked on my roles or tasks in my group.

☐ I marked places I didn't understand or wanted to discuss with my group.

☐ I used technology to assist in my reading and understanding of the book.

☐ I participated and completed my assignments on time.

My overall rating of myself: _____

_____

_____

_____

_____

The person who I think should get the best grade within my group is

_____ I think so because he or she did the following:

_____

_____

_____

_____

_____

_____

_____

Table A.2

Literature Circles: Self-Assessment of Discussion

Name: _____ Circle: _____

Book: _____ Page: _____

Contribution	Example	Teacher's Score
I shared my ideas and suggestions with my circle or group.		
I encouraged other members of the group to participate.		
I spoke clearly enough to be understood by all members.		
I summarized or repeated my ideas when necessary.		
I respectfully answered others' questions.		
I respected others: when I disagreed I did not hurt others feelings.		
I listened courteously and without unnecessary interruptions.		
I remained on topic and stayed focused.		

My most important contribution to the literature circle was: _____

_____

_____

How I can improve for the next discussion: _____

_____

_____

Table A.3

Literature Circles: Journal Scoring Rubric

Individual Grades	Progressing —not yet target	Target	Exemplary
Response Journal	Journal indicates student: Has not read text carefully—student cannot identify main ideas or interpret text. Missing reflections—one or more of the required journal prompts have not been addressed. Cannot identify specific examples of growth in under-standing the text. Cannot clearly state the contribution he or she made to the group discussion.	Journal indicates student: Has grasped main ideas. Can offer reasonable reflections and interpretations, although may have some incomplete or questionable reflections and interpretations. Has addressed all required journal prompts. Provides at least two specific examples, demonstrating a richer or better understanding after group discussion. Can state his or her contribution to the group.	Journal indicates student: Has achieved genuine insights as evidenced by reflect-ions and interpretations of text. Has gained richer understanding of the text through group discussion. Evaluates effectiveness of his or her own contribution to group discussion.
Work Habits	Deadlines are not met. Journal entries are often missing. Student needs reminders to stay on task or distracts other students. Frequently not actively involved in discussion group. Lack of productivity or ability to work within the discussion group.	Deadlines are met, and journal is complete. Journal entries are available at start of class. Student is usually on-task, does not distract other groups, and needs little direction from the teacher. Works well in discussion group: is productive and cooperative.	Student's work is on time and did not need reminding from the teacher. Encourages other group members to keep focused on the task. Student is focused and productive—took collaborative work seriously.

Table A.4

Literature Circles: Role Sheet Scoring Rubric

Individual Grades	Progressing —not yet target	Target	Exemplary
Role Sheet– Job Aid	Student is not prepared for Literature Circle. Discussion material was not read. Role sheets/job aids were not done or not completed.	Student has read text carefully. Role sheet/ job aid is complete. Responses to assigned tasks on role indicate that student has an adequate understanding of the material.	Responses to assigned tasks indicate that student has achieved a superior or unique understanding of the material read.
Work Habits	Deadlines are not met. Role sheets are often missing or incomplete. Student needs reminders to stay on task or distracts other students. Frequently not actively involved in discussion group. Lack of productivity or ability to work within the discussion group.	Role sheets are always available at start of the group discussion. Deadlines are met. Role Sheets/job aids are complete. Student is usually on-task, does not distract other groups, and needs little direction from the teacher. Works well in discussion group: is productive and cooperative.	Student's work is on time and student did not need reminding from the teacher. Encourages other group members to keep focused on the task. Student is focused and productive—took collaborative work seriously.

Table A.5

Literature Circle Rubric

To be evaluated by the Discussion Coordinator:
Daily Participation Scoring Guide for_____Discussion Group

Role	Was student prepared for discussion?
Discussion Coordinator	☐ Yes ☐ No Comments:
Vocabulary Elaborator	☐ Yes ☐ No Comments:
Literary Expositor	☐ Yes ☐ No Comments:
Graphic Illustrator	☐ Yes ☐ No Comments:
Graphic Organizer	☐ Yes ☐ No Comments:
Background Researcher	☐ Yes ☐ No Comments:
Web Researcher	☐ Yes ☐ No Comments:
Media Hunter	☐ Yes ☐ No Comments:
Connector	☐ Yes ☐ No Comments:
Mapper/ Tracker	☐ Yes ☐ No Comments:

Index